Early praise for *Programming WebAssembly with Rust*

Concise and well-paced, this book quickly dives into the details of WebAssembly, letting readers get their hands dirty building interesting Wasm applications. It's loaded with great examples and touches on many different aspects of programming while paving the trail for WebAssembly development.

➤ **Sean Boyle**
Senior Software Engineer, Cerner

Programming WebAssembly with Rust is a great resource for learning a low-level language (WebAssembly) and showing how its power can be harnessed with Rust. It is perfect for people who like to understand how things work.

➤ **Jason Pike**
Software Development Coach, Sigao Studios

Starting with a detailed look at WebAssembly internals and the WAST language before moving on to solving fun gaming problems with Rust and Wasm, *Programming WebAssembly with Rust* ensures readers gain a foundational knowledge of WebAssembly and have fun doing so.

➤ **Balaji Sivaraman**
Senior Technology Consultant, ThoughtWorks

I read *Programming WebAssembly with Rust* hardly knowing anything about either. I came away planning to make some time to build a WebAssembly module and publish to an npm registry—and with a clear idea of how to do so. An enjoyable read which suggests some mind-bending possibilities for the future of the web.

➤ **Stephen Wolff**
Director, Max Gate Digital Ltd.

Programming WebAssembly with Rust

Unified Development for Web, Mobile, and Embedded Applications

Kevin Hoffman

The Pragmatic Bookshelf

Raleigh, North Carolina

Many of the designations used by manufacturers and sellers to distinguish their products are claimed as trademarks. Where those designations appear in this book, and The Pragmatic Programmers, LLC was aware of a trademark claim, the designations have been printed in initial capital letters or in all capitals. The Pragmatic Starter Kit, The Pragmatic Programmer, Pragmatic Programming, Pragmatic Bookshelf, PragProg and the linking *g* device are trademarks of The Pragmatic Programmers, LLC.

Every precaution was taken in the preparation of this book. However, the publisher assumes no responsibility for errors or omissions, or for damages that may result from the use of information (including program listings) contained herein.

Our Pragmatic books, screencasts, and audio books can help you and your team create better software and have more fun. Visit us at *https://pragprog.com*.

The team that produced this book includes:

Publisher: Andy Hunt
VP of Operations: Janet Furlow
Managing Editor: Susan Conant
Development Editor: Andrea Stewart
Copy Editor: Jasmine Kwityn
Indexing: Potomac Indexing, LLC
Layout: Gilson Graphics

For sales, volume licensing, and support, please contact *support@pragprog.com*.

For international rights, please contact *rights@pragprog.com*.

ISBN-13: 978-1-68050-636-5
Book version: P1.0—March 2019

For my grandfather—Walter K. MacAdam—
inventor, tinkerer, and IEEE president. He
quietly supported my exposure to computers
and programming throughout my childhood,
often in ways I didn't know until after his death.
I always wanted to grow up to be like him, and
I only wish he could've seen this book.

Contents

Part III — Working with Non-Web Hosts

Acknowledgments

This book would not have been possible without the infinite patience and support of my wife, who has far more faith in me than I do.

I would also like to thank all of the technical reviewers for keeping me honest and accurate: Vijay Raghavan Aravamudhan, Jacob Chae, Nick Fitzgerald, Peter Perlepes, Jason Pike, Sean Boyle, Martjin Reuvers, Balaji Sivaraman, and Stephen Wolff.

Introduction

I'm old enough to have lived through quite a few seismic changes in the way developers build software and the kinds of products we can build. I was just starting my career when DPMI gave us native access to 32-bit integers, allowed unfettered access to a heap greater than 640k, and enabled the creation of ground-breaking games like *DOOM*. I remember the potential behind Java's promise of *write once, run anywhere*. I was there when small, local communities built around dial-up bulletin board systems (BBSes) faded as the world became a single, digital community riding the wave of the Internet's surge toward ubiquity. I experienced the shift in solution design from client/server to fat server to fat client and back again, today landing on *cloud native* applications, microservices, and independent functions where everything including our infrastructure is a service.

I remember the web's growth from a billion archipelagos of text (often blinking!) and Under Construction signs where the coolest places were the ones with the most intricate full-page background images, to the vast, sprawling engine of commerce, communication, lifestyle, and social connection that it is today. The web has gone from a place where only an elite few dabbled in that strange new world to a place where millions of people spend their days coding some of the most powerful and complex applications of the modern era.

I firmly believe that we stand on the precipice of another seismic change— *WebAssembly*. This new technology holds within it the potential to radically change how developers build applications for the web. Moreover, as you'll see throughout this book, WebAssembly is more than just a new pebble thrown into the ocean of web technologies. It's a tsunami that can change not only how consumers interact with and how developers build applications but also fundamentally alter the kinds of applications we can create. It may even transform our core definition of the word *application*.

Today's Web Technology

Today's web is a veritable playground for developers. You have the luxury of easy access to broadband speeds (with exceptions). Browsers are faster and more powerful than they've ever been, and the workstations people use to run those browsers have oodles of RAM, storage, and multiple cores—even the mobile devices.

Today's JavaScript is nothing like the primordial 1995 JavaScript that drew so much ire from the developer community. It dominates the web development landscape so much that its own ubiquity has become something of a joke or a meme. Competition between browser vendors (they didn't call it the *browser wars* for nothing) has spurred years of refining the way their products execute JavaScript, which will be a key discussion point when you get into the details of browser-hosted WebAssembly.

Modern browsers have virtual machines responsible for JavaScript execution. Internally they optimize and produce a form of bytecode from processed JavaScript. This, coupled with more memory and processing power, means that JavaScript is actually *fast*. Not just a little bit fast, but it's so fast you can play full, grade-A video games in the browser. Applications can perform complex calculations, run machine learning models, process vast amounts of data, and otherwise treat the browser like an operating system.

Frameworks like *React*, *Angular*, *Backbone*, *VueJS*, and countless others have made a dramatic impact on how web applications are built. Modern web applications can render incredibly dense user interfaces like what you see on Facebook or YouTube, all while receiving real-time events published from servers in the cloud to provide a level of interaction that's now such a ubiquitous feature that web sites that don't provide this new level of real-time interaction are often publicly shamed and doomed to fail.

Nothing in the rest of this book that extols the virtues of WebAssembly should take away from the fact that the modern, programmable web is a giant virtual toy store, ripe for the plundering by eager developers. For any avid learner of technology, it's a great time to be alive (and probably learn some JavaScript).

The Tech of Tomorrow

WebAssembly is currently a 1.0 product, having just reached its first MVP (Minimum Viable Product). As with most 1.0 products, it's bound to experience some growing pains and points of friction, and we'll go over those in depth as they come up in this book. As you look at the current state of WebAssembly and its limitations, you might get discouraged and feel the urge to give up and wait for things to get more mature. But I think the time is right to start learning and developing with this incredible new technology, and there are already many WebAssembly 1.0 products deployed and running in the wild and more appearing every day. In the span between two edits of this chapter, someone released a virtual machine built in WebAssembly that runs Windows 95 in a browser.

The good news is that the experience will only improve over time. The tooling will get better, the interface between the browser and WebAssembly modules will get better, support for non-browser hosts will get better, and the number of tested and proven use cases will grow. In short, as time goes on, every aspect of the development of WebAssembly modules will improve.

I am convinced that WebAssembly is at the tip of the next wave of truly paradigm-shifting changes in the programmable Internet. I did indeed mean to say *Internet* and not just *web*. The distinction might seem subtle, but I'm also thoroughly convinced that the browser as a host for WebAssembly modules is just the tip of the iceberg. WebAssembly is going to join the long line of game-changing innovations in the history of the Internet and fundamentally alter our concept of applications.

Who This Book Is For

This book is for anyone who wants to build web applications. Whether you have had just a little bit of JavaScript exposure or whether you are a seasoned professional with dozens of React and Redux applications under your belt, WebAssembly has the potential to change the way that you build apps and the power of those applications in a way that few technologies before ever have.

Whether you consider yourself a front-end, back-end, embedded, or any other kind of developer—this book is for you. Compiling other languages to WebAssembly means you get to use familiar development life cycles and toolchains and build and test strongly-typed, powerful code.

Finally, if you think that there is more to this WebAssembly thing than just the web applications, then you will enjoy this book as well as we build WebAssembly interpreters in Rust and run them on Raspberry Pis to control hardware via GPIO. WebAssembly holds a lot of promise for many different types of developers, including the promise of unifying back- and front-end coding experiences.

Why Rust?

Rust is a systems language that compiles to native binaries on any number of operating systems and hardware architectures. It is fast, its binaries take up very little space and have a small memory footprint, and is designed from the ground up to avoid accidental mutation, null referencing, and data races. In fact, the compiler will check your code and prevent you from making those mistakes.

But I chose Rust for this book for reasons beyond just the language syntax and its powerful compiler. What excited me about Rust was how quickly it embraced WebAssembly. While other languages right now can compile code to WebAssembly, the sheer number of libraries and tools available within the Rust community for WebAssembly is staggering. It is the enthusiasm, support, and rapid pace of advancement in the Rust WebAssembly community that influenced my decision to use Rust for this book.

What You'll Learn

This book is divided up into three main parts:

Building a Foundation

As you build a foundation, you'll learn the fundamentals and the core architecture of WebAssembly, including what it can and cannot do and how you can develop basic applications. By the time you reach the end of this section, you'll be able to create a Checkers engine written entirely in raw WebAssembly.

Interacting with JavaScript

Building on your solid WebAssembly foundation, you'll move on to using Rust to create your WebAssembly modules. You'll start with the basics of creating a Rust version of your Checkers engine, and then you'll move on to using code generation, advanced tooling, and macros to build powerful web applications that interact with JavaScript. By the end of this section, you'll be able to write a multiuser, real-time chat application in Rust that compiles to WebAssembly.

Working with Non-Web Hosts

Once you've had your first taste of the power of WebAssembly, it's time to take it to the next level and start working with non-web hosts.

WebAssembly is about far more than just building things for the web, and you'll see this firsthand as you create modules that control LED patterns for lights attached to a Raspberry Pi and, as your final project, you create a fully multiplayer arena battle game that lets developers pit their WebAssembly code against each other in a battle to the death.

Now it's time to get coding!

Part I

Building a Foundation

Let's get started by exploring WebAssembly fundamentals and learn how to write raw WebAssembly code.

CHAPTER 1

WebAssembly Fundamentals

With WebAssembly, there is a symbiotic relationship between the compiled WebAssembly binary (called a *module*) and the host responsible for interpreting it. This relationship is at the heart of everything that you can do with this new technology, and understanding where the boundaries are between module and host is key to being able to build effective WebAssembly applications.

WebAssembly can be viewed at two different levels—the raw, foundational level and at the higher level of other programming languages using WebAssembly as a target. Before you can understand and appreciate what languages like Rust are doing when they produce WebAssembly modules, you'll need to know what WebAssembly can do, what it can't, and how to use language-independent tools.

This chapter gets you started at the foundation level, giving you an overview of what WebAssembly is, how it works, and how other features can be built upon this foundation. By the end of this chapter, you'll be able to create and build your own WebAssembly modules using cross-platform language tools and your favorite code editor. While what you learn in these first few chapters may not be things you do on a daily basis, the context they provide will be invaluable as you build real applications with WebAssembly.

Introducing WebAssembly

If the modern programmable web is merely a toy store, then WebAssembly is a toy warehouse filled with toys as far as the eye can see. Developers who spend most of their time working on the front end often long for some of the features, testability, and constraints prevalent in the world of servers and services. Likewise, folks who spend most of their time toiling behind the counter, away from the customer but carefully assembling all the parts of their order, often long for the fluid, expressive, blank canvas world the front end represents. People who work in both worlds are keenly aware of the paradigm differences between the two and why the grass isn't always greener on the other side.

What if "sides" or "front" or "back" didn't matter anymore? What if there was a new way of doing things, where you could write loosely coupled business logic that flows between servers, services, clients, and browsers without any shenanigans? What if you could have the best parts of the front- and back-end worlds and still choose the most appropriate language for your problems?

By the time you reach the end of this book, you'll have learned enough about WebAssembly development that these propositions won't sound like they came from a snake-oil salesman. They'll ring true and hopefully inspire you to start building amazing new WebAssembly applications.

What Is WebAssembly?

The WebAssembly home page[1] says that it is a binary instruction format for a stack-based virtual machine. *Wasm* (a contraction, not an acronym, for WebAssembly) is designed to be *portable* (capable of running on different OSes, architectures, and environments without modification), and used as a compilation target for higher-level languages like C++, Rust, Go, and many others. The website also claims that Wasm enables deployment on the web for client and server applications alike.

Let's pick this definition apart a bit, because it's rather dense.

First, and most importantly, WebAssembly is a *portable binary instruction format*. This is very similar to the original intent behind Java's bytecode and, if you're familiar with the .NET Framework, you may recognize this concept as implemented in *ILASM*, the low-level instruction set supporting the Common Language Runtime. You'll see this in depth in the next chapter, but for now it should suffice to know that the operations encoded in a WebAssembly module are not tightly coupled to any one hardware architecture or operating system, and these operations are just codes that a parser knows how to interpret.

Next, there's the phrase *stack-based virtual machine*. We'll go over this in detail soon, but the short explanation is that this stack machine simultaneously contributes to WebAssembly's tremendous speed, power, and several of its limitations.

---

1. webassembly.org

Finally, there's a spot in the definition on which I fundamentally disagree. The phrase "deployment on the web" might limit your thinking and your imagination. This is a portable format that can run *anywhere* you can build a *host*, which you'll also be learning about later. Limiting WebAssembly's scope to the web (despite its name) does it a disservice.

What WebAssembly Is Not

The first question I get asked once I get on my WebAssembly soapbox is, "Isn't Wasm just another transpile target for JS?" *Transpiling* is translating from one high-level source language to another high-level source language. This is in contrast to the usual compiling, which takes a high-level source language and translates it into a low-level machine code. For example, converting TypeScript or React JSX into browser-executable JavaScript is done through transpiling. WebAssembly is *not* a JavaScript transpile target (though you can actually compile *TypeScript* into a Wasm module if you're into that sort of thing).

WebAssembly is also *not* meant to replace JavaScript. This is somewhat of a controversial opinion, as a large group of WebAssembly devotees online are convinced that it represents the death knell of JavaScript. While it might signal the beginning of a new era in which you write significantly less *manual* JavaScript, you still need JS to host WebAssembly 1.0 in the browser.

It's also not intended as a mere replacement for (or successor to) Flash, Silverlight, Adobe AIR, or Java Applets. As you'll discover, WebAssembly isn't run as a process outside the browser. How seamlessly it integrates with the user experience is entirely up to the developer and the tools they use.

Another important thing to remember is that WebAssembly, on its own, isn't a programming language. While there is both a binary and a text format, writing it by hand for anything beyond a few samples would take far too long and be too difficult to test and troubleshoot. Knowing how to write it by hand, however, will help you make the right decisions as you learn to build WebAssembly applications with *Rust*.

WebAssembly doesn't stand on its own. Like a game cartridge without a console or a BluRay disc without a player, it's incomplete in isolation. Much like a symbiote that needs to feed off of its host to survive, WebAssembly can't interact with anything outside the bounds of its own sandbox unless the host allows it. All I/O and other interactions are done entirely at the behest of the host such as a browser or a console application. While this might sound like an unfair limitation, you'll see a number of times throughout this book why this is actually a good thing.

Try It Out

The best way to start learning something is to jump right in. Imagine one of those ball pits kids get to play in but, sadly, us adults are usually forbidden. As learners, our first exposure to new material is like jumping into this pit, surrounded by a dizzying array of colors and buried up to our necks in confusion. As we struggle to make our way to the far end of the ball pit, we gradually get our footing, the colors become more familiar, the shape and landscape of the ball pit gets smaller, and we're able to reason about it. After a while, we crawl out of the pit, having learned enough that we're eager to jump back in and discover more.

For WebAssembly, you're going to jump into the ball pit by using an online tool called *WebAssembly Studio*. In December 2017, *Mozilla* started working on this project as a way to provide a low-friction introduction to WebAssembly. It's a combination of some of their other WebAssembly tools like *WasmFiddle*.[2] This tool is entirely online and lets you create new projects in C, Rust, or *AssemblyScript*, a tool for compiling TypeScript to WebAssembly. It has gone through bursts of community activity and contribution since its creation.

Open up your browser (any up-to-date version of Firefox, Edge, Chrome, or Safari should work) and point it at webassembly.studio. You'll come to a screen that presents the following options for creating a new project:

- Empty C Project
- Empty Rust Project
- Empty AssemblyScript Project
- Hello World in C
- Hello World Rust Project

Choose "Empty Rust Project" and then click the Create button. This will create a new project within WebAssembly Studio, including a README.md file, a src directory, and the file you want to explore: main.rs. You'll see the following code:

```
#[no_mangle]
pub extern "C" fn add_one(x: i32) -> i32 {
  x + 1
}
```

---

2.   wasdk.github.io/WasmFiddle/

The WebAssembly Studio site, with its almost entirely black color scheme, doesn't make for print-friendly screenshots so none have been included here.

If you're familiar with Rust, then this should be self-explanatory. If you're new to Rust, don't worry—you'll spend quite a bit of time working through Rust's syntax throughout the book. This code listing defines a function that adds 1 to a 32-bit signed integer, returning that value in a signed 32-bit integer. Believe it or not, this code can produce a WebAssembly module.

Using Rust's no_mangle macro tells the compiler not to change the signature of the function during compilation. As you'll see in upcoming chapters, there are some aspects of executing WebAssembly that require some naming conventions.

Click the Build and Run button and you'll see the blue bar on the bottom of the editor flash. Then, the white square canvas in the bottom right-hand corner will display the number *42*.

Congratulations, you've just written, compiled, and executed your first WebAssembly module. Where did the number 42 come from? Take a look at the main.js file by clicking on it in your browser:

```
fetch('../out/main.wasm').then(response =>
  response.arrayBuffer()
).then(bytes => WebAssembly.instantiate(bytes)).then(results => {
  instance = results.instance;
  document.getElementById("container").innerText = instance.exports.add_one(41);
}).catch(console.error);
```

Don't worry if some of this JavaScript looks unfamiliar to you—it'll be second nature by the time we're done. The indicated line of code invokes the add_one function in the WebAssembly module and places the result value inside the container DOM element. And now you've built a WebAssembly module that adds 1 to any number. It might not be all that impressive, but you've taken that first leap into WebAssembly.

The pattern of writing Rust code, compiling to WebAssembly, and then running the module in a browser is one that you'll repeat many times throughout this book. For now, though, let's take a step back from this code and take a look at what makes WebAssembly tick so you can have a better idea of what's happening in the preceding example.

Understanding WebAssembly Architecture

In this section, you'll get a good look inside the engine that makes WebAssembly work. Its unique architecture makes it incredibly powerful, portable, and efficient—though this power comes with some limitations.

Stack Machines

The type of computer that you're using right now is likely a *Register Machine*. Laptops, desktops, mobile devices, virtual machines, even microcontrollers and embedded devices are register machines. A register machine is a machine (physical or virtual) where the processor instructions explicitly refer to certain registers, or data storage locations, on the processor. Accessing these registers is fast and efficient because the data is available directly within the CPU.

For example, if you want to add two numbers together, you'd use the ADD instruction and you'd pass it the names of two registers as parameters, as shown in this bit of x86 assembly:

```
ADD al, ah
```

In the preceding code, the values contained in ah and al will be added together, with the result stored in al.

WebAssembly is a *stack machine*. In a stack machine, most of the instructions assume that the operands are sitting on the stack, rather than stored in specified registers. The WebAssembly stack is a LIFO (Last In, First Out) stack. If you're unfamiliar with the concept of a stack: it is as its name implies— values are piled (stacked) on top of each other, and unlike arrays where you can access any data regardless of location in the pile, stacks only allow you to pop data off or push data onto the top.

To add two numbers in a stack machine, you *push* those numbers onto the top of the stack. Then you push the ADD instruction onto the stack. The two operands and the instruction are then popped off the top and the result of the addition is pushed on in their place.

There are a number of advantages to a stack machine that made it an appealing choice for WebAssembly: their small binary size, efficient instruction coding, and ease of portability just to name a few.

There are some fairly well-known stack machines, including the *Java Virtual Machine* (JVM) and the bytecode executor for the .NET *Common Language Runtime*. In the case of those virtual machines, developers are spared the effort of writing assembly or thinking in prefix or Polish[3] (where the operator comes first) notation because of the intermediate steps and code generation happening behind the scenes.

Data Types

Admit it—you've been spoiled. Modern programming languages with hashes, lists, arrays, sets, extra-large numbers, and tuples have spoiled you. These languages also probably let you create your own types through structs or classes. Some of them even let you overload operators, and some of those overloads can even work on custom types. The world is your oyster and you have few limits. That is not the world of WebAssembly. As their name should imply, *assembly* languages are designed to be made up of primitives that can be used as building blocks by higher level languages.

WebAssembly 1.0 has exactly four data types:

Type	Description
i32	32-Bit Integer
i64	64-Bit Integer
f32	32-Bit Floating-Point Number
f64	64-Bit Floating-Point Number

One aspect of this relatively limited set of data types is that WebAssembly doesn't assign any intrinsic signed-ness to numbers as they're stored. The assumption of whether a number is signed or unsigned is only performed at the time of an operation. For example, while there's only one i32 data type, there are signed and unsigned versions of that type's arithmetic operators, e.g. i32.add and i32.add_u.

When you're using a high-level language that compiles to WebAssembly on your behalf, you shouldn't have to worry about this subtlety. But when you're writing raw Wasm in the text format by hand, it could trip you up in unexpected ways.

Control Flow

WebAssembly's handling of control flow is a little different than other, less portable assembly languages. WebAssembly goes to great lengths to ensure that its control flow can't invalidate type safety, and can't be hijacked by attackers even with a "heap corruption"[4]-style attack in linear memory. For

---

3. en.wikipedia.org/wiki/Polish_notation
4. https://pdfs.semanticscholar.org/14f1/4b032235c345dfb3b3ecc8a879bbe4072407.pdf

example, many assembly languages allow easily exploited blind jump instructions, whereas you'll discover that WebAssembly does not. This additional layer of safety pairs well with the safety-first philosophy of Rust.

Wasm control flow is accomplished the same way everything else is within a stack machine—by pushing things onto, and popping things off of, the stack. For example, with an if instruction, if whatever is at the top of the stack evaluates as true (non-zero), then the if branch will be executed.

Take a look at an example of the if statement in action:

```
(if (i32.eq (call $getHealth) (i32.const 0))
  (then (call $doDeath))
  (else (call $stillAlive))
)
```

In this code, if our hypothetical player's health has reached 0, then we'll call the doDeath function, otherwise we'll call the stillAlive function. All those seemingly extra parentheses will make sense later in the chapter.

WebAssembly has the following control flow instructions available:

Instruction	Description
if	Marks the beginning of an if branching instruction.
else	Marks the else block of an if instruction
loop	A labeled block used to create loops
block	A sequence of instructions, often used within expressions
br	Branch to the given label in a containing instruction or block
br_if	Identical to a branch, but with a prerequisite condition
br_table	Branches, but instead of to a label it jumps to a function index in a table
return	Returns a value from the instruction (1.0 only supports one return value)
end	Marks the end of a block, loop, if, or a function
nop	No self-respecting assembly language is without an operation that does nothing

Linear Memory

As you work with linear memory, you'll truly begin to appreciate the extent to which modern high-level languages have spoiled you. With most languages, you can quickly and easily create a new instance of something on the heap with an operator like new.

Internally, the compiler knows the size of this thing (or has some trick to compensate for not knowing). When you pass an instance of something to a function, the compiler knows whether you're passing a pointer or a value and how to arrange that value on your stack or heap in order to make the data available to a function.

WebAssembly doesn't have a heap in the traditional sense. There's no concept of a new operator. In fact, you don't allocate memory at the object level because there are no objects. There's also no garbage collection (at least not in the 1.0 MVP).

Instead, WebAssembly has *linear memory*. This is a contiguous block of bytes that can be declared internally within the module, exported out of a module, or imported from the host. Think of it as though the code you're writing is restricted to using a single variable that is a byte array. Your WebAssembly module can grow the linear memory block in increments called *pages* of 64KB if it needs more space. Sadly, determining if you need more space is entirely up to you and your code—there's no runtime to do this for you.

This image with variables and byte offsets illustrates just one way to store data in a block of linear memory (how you choose to use and fill linear memory is entirely up to you and your code):

var1 [0...39]	var2 [40...79]	var3 [80...119]	unused

In addition to the efficiency of direct memory access, there's another reason why it's ideal for WebAssembly: *security*. While the host can read and write any linear memory given to a Wasm module at any time, the Wasm module can never access any of the host's memory.

Direct DOM Access Is an Illusion

If you've seen WebAssembly demos that look like they're directly accessing the browser DOM from inside the module—that's an illusion. The host and module are sharing a block of linear memory, and the host is choosing to execute bespoke JavaScript to translate the contents of that shared memory area into updates to the DOM, just like you saw at the beginning of this chapter. This may change in future versions of WebAssembly, but for now, this remains little more than smoke and mirrors.

As you'll see in the coming chapters, linear memory is crucial to being able to create powerful applications with WebAssembly. Before using high-level languages like Rust, you should learn how to manipulate linear memory manually so you can appreciate the extent of the work done on your behalf by tools and code generation and understand the impact of your designs.

Building a WebAssembly Application

At the beginning of this chapter, you built and ran a simple Rust-based WebAssembly application using WebAssembly studio. In this section, you'll install some tools on your machine that will allow you to compile and interpret WebAssembly modules.

Installing the WebAssembly Binary Toolkit

The WebAssembly Binary Toolkit (pronounced "wabbit") is a general-purpose set of command-line tools you'll use for building, examining, and troubleshooting WebAssembly modules. Whether you're on Windows, Mac, or Linux, the first thing you're going to need to install is *CMake*.[5]

Installing CMake varies widely across operating systems, so you'll need to check the instructions specific to your platform. Come back and continue with the wabt installation once you've verified that CMake is up and running locally.

Next, follow the instructions on the wabt[6] GitHub repository README to complete the installation. You should be able to get the binaries from a release, but if you want to build the toolkit yourself, go ahead and simply run make install and then, after a fairly lengthy compilation process, you'll see a bunch of executables in the bin directory beneath wherever you checked out the repository, including some or all of the following:

- wasm2c
- wasm2wat
- wasm-interp
- wasm-objdump
- wasm-opcodecnt
- wasm-validate
- wast2json
- wat2wasm
- wat-desugar

The exact list of files may have changed since this book was published, but you'll at the very least need wat2wasm and wasm-objdump for the next section where you will be writing real WebAssembly code. Make sure that you can

---

5. cmake.org
6. github.com/WebAssembly/wabt

execute both of these commands in a terminal or a shell and get the help text before continuing on.

On my machine, make install installed all of the compiled binaries in /usr/local/bin:

```
-- Install configuration: "Debug"
-- Installing: /usr/local/bin/wat2wasm
-- Installing: /usr/local/bin/wast2json
-- Installing: /usr/local/bin/wasm2wat
-- Installing: /usr/local/bin/wasm2c
-- Installing: /usr/local/bin/wasm-opcodecnt
-- Installing: /usr/local/bin/wasm-objdump
-- Installing: /usr/local/bin/wasm-interp
-- Installing: /usr/local/bin/spectest-interp
-- Installing: /usr/local/bin/wat-desugar
-- Installing: /usr/local/bin/wasm-validate
-- Installing: /usr/local/bin/wabt-unittests
```

Coding in the WebAssembly Text Format

Before I launch into an arguably dense and detailed section of fairly low-level coding, I want to answer the question of *why*. Why should you spend the effort learning how to write raw wast when you've got modern compilers that can do it for you?

I don't like *magic*. I don't like black boxes that do things I don't understand. I am put off when I have to use a third-party system when I don't understand its internal workings, or at least the motivations behind the decisions made in the building of the thing.

You could go forward and build powerful WebAssembly applications and live your life without knowing how it all works inside. However, I contend that this chapter and its contents provide the foundation on which a solid WebAssembly development practice should be built. You could, in theory, skip this chapter. But, as Morpheus told Neo in *The Matrix*, "You take the red pill—you stay in Wonderland and I show you how deep the rabbit-hole goes."

When we get into the chapters on building alternative, non-browser hosts for WebAssembly modules, you will absolutely benefit from the knowledge and experience gained in this chapter.

The physical process of writing code in the WebAssembly Text Format (.wat files) is pretty easy—just open up your favorite text editor (VSCode, Atom, and others all have syntax highlighters for WebAssembly) and start typing.

As you now know, WebAssembly doesn't have a string data type. This makes the canonical "Hello, World" sample a little difficult. In fact, the code required to actually produce that output in a browser is pretty complicated. If you try to go this route as your first exposure to writing *wat*, you're likely to get discouraged.

For a simpler example that takes advantage of WebAssembly's simple data types, let's try creating a module with a single function that adds two numbers together and returns the result. Open up your text editor and create the add1.wat file with the following contents:

```
fundamentals/add1.wat
(module
  (func $add (param $lhs i32) (param $rhs i32) (result i32)
    get_local $lhs
    get_local $rhs
    i32.add)
  (export "add" (func $add))
)
```

The first expression at the top of every module is the module declaration. Note that there's no module name, package name, or namespace. There are a number of other things that can go below this declaration, but in this case, you're just creating a single function, marked by the func keyword. Each parameter to a function is indicated with an S-expression[7] (a parenthesized syntax for representing data or code as nested trees, first created for Lisp) in the following form:

```
(param $parametername datatype)
```

In this case, there are two 32-bit integer parameters: $lhs and $rhs and the result will be a 32-bit integer.

The call to get_local retrieves a function-scoped value and places it on the Wasm execution stack. In this function, you're calling get_local twice, putting the two parameters on the stack, and then calling i32.add. This adds the two values on the stack, pops them off, and puts the sum in their place. The value left on the stack at the end of the function is the default return value.

The order these instructions appear in the code can seem awkward. This is pure postfix (operator-last) notation and makes for some difficult reading. You don't necessarily have to do it this way. There's an alternative, pure S-expression prefix notation where you put the operation first and operands second, as you see in this code:

---

7.   en.wikipedia.org/wiki/S-expression

```
fundamentals/add2.wat
(module
  (func $add (param $lhs i32) (param $rhs i32) (result i32)
    (i32.add
        (get_local $lhs)
        (get_local $rhs)
    )
  )
  (export "add" (func $add))
)
```

In the second form, there are more parentheses, but the code is easier to read, especially as you get into more complicated patterns like those in the next chapter. I'll be using the second form from now on.

To invoke this function in WebAssembly, you use the call keyword, as shown in this code that adds 9 and 5:

```
(call $add (i32.const 5) (i32.const 9))
```

Using the Binary Toolkit

Now that you've got some source code, it's time to compile it and do some exploration with the "wabbit" tools. Go to the directory where you created add1.wat and run the following commands (wat2wasm should be in your path):

```
$ wat2wasm add1.wat -o add.wasm
$ wat2wasm add2.wat -o add_sexpr.wasm
```

If everything goes according to plan, you'll receive the "no news is good news" response—*nothing*. Next, use wasm-objdump to get a look at what actually made it into your compiled add.wasm file. The *-x* option adds extra detail to the output:

```
$ wasm-objdump add.wasm -x

add.wasm:       file format wasm 0x1

Section Details:

Type:
 - type[0] (i32, i32) -> i32
Function:
 - func[0] sig=0 <add>
Export:
 - func[0] <add> -> "add"
```

There's some pretty good information here. You can tell that there's a function type declared that accepts two integers and returns an integer. There's a function at index 0 called add. Finally, there's an export called add.

It is important to keep in mind that you can create functions in a WebAssembly module and not export them. In fact, functions are all private to the module and remain unexported until you explicitly write an export statement. If you run the same object dump command on add_sexpr.wasm, you'll see the exact same type and exports.

There's one last thing worth exploring—take a look at what the code looks like after a round trip when you convert the binary add_sexpr.wasm file to its corresponding text format:

```
$ wasm2wat add_sexpr.wasm -o roundtrip.wat
```

fundamentals/roundtrip.wat
```
(module
  (type (;0;) (func (param i32 i32) (result i32)))
  (func (;0;) (type 0) (param i32 i32) (result i32)
    get_local 0
    get_local 1
    i32.add)
  (export "add" (func 0)))
```

Here you can see that there's a type created, a function of that data type, and then the instructions have reverted to the inverted stack notation rather than the instruction-first version. Finally, you can see that the export now just refers to the function at index 0 rather than a name. The separation of the symbol name and the function index is part of what ensures this kind of round-trip compilation is possible.

The reason this round trip is important is to show what WebAssembly might look like when produced by other languages, and, just in case you had any doubts, to prove that your code is truly portable and can be opened, disassembled, and re-generated at will. This also means anyone with access to these tools can see *everything* inside your WebAssembly module—a point to take note of when it comes to design and security in the future.

WebAssembly Source Maps

If a web browser has access to both the binary format and the original source code, then you can expose a *source map* through the developer tools. Even at this early stage in the technology's life, you can already set breakpoints within WebAssembly modules written in Rust running in Firefox. When the respective line of code comes up, the browser renders the original (non-wat) code via the source map and not the minified code that you saw in the round-trip file.

Wrapping Up

In this chapter, you got your first real exposure to writing WebAssembly code. You got the "wabbit" toolkit installed and you used it to compile, examine, and disassemble WebAssembly modules. You've received a preliminary exposure to the syntax and specifications for WebAssembly and you should be able to experiment with creating your own very basic modules.

In the next chapter, you'll build on what you've learned so far to create a fully functioning game with just the basic WebAssembly tools.

*...the imagination is unleashed by constraints. You break out
of the box by stepping into shackles.*

> *Jonah Lehrer*

CHAPTER 2

Building WebAssembly Checkers

Sample applications small enough to fit into a quick blog post are very good at giving you a quick, painless introduction to some new piece of syntax. They show you how to print to the console, they show you how many parentheses you might normally need for a given line of code, and you get to see working code so long as you don't mind lacking the context of the surrounding application not shown in the post.

Even when full applications are created, the nature of the easily consumed medium means that these illustrative applications often look *nothing* like real-world applications, and they bear little to no resemblance to anything you might deploy to production.

In this chapter, you won't be creating a contrived "Hello, World" WebAssembly module. Instead, you'll be creating a module that can be used to run a game of checkers (also called *draughts* depending on which part of the world you are from).

You'll build this module by creating a series of small functions that, once complete, will work together to provide the fundamentals of a working checkers game. There's always a trade-off between the complexity of a real application and the need to keep an example simple enough to be used as a learning tool, so we cut a few corners on evaluating some game rules and edge cases, but the code will be playable when you're done.

Playing Checkers, the Board Game

If you've played checkers, then you can probably skip this section. If you need a refresher, then this will still be a quick read.

Checkers is a fairly simple game played on an 8×8 game board. The board's squares are typically alternating colors (one of the most common in the US is a black and red board).

Each player then positions 12 pieces on the board in fixed squares spaced evenly one square apart from each other. One player controls the black pieces and another controls the white (or red) pieces. The player controlling the black pieces makes the first move.

The simplest move is where a piece is allowed to slide diagonally on the board if there is no other player occupying that spot. If there is, you might be able to *jump* and capture that player's piece. Players take turns moving or jumping (which can include multiple jumps per turn if pieces are positioned right) until one player reaches the opponent's home row. This row is called the *kings row* or *crownhead*. Once in the opponent's kings row, the player's piece is *crowned* and gains the ability to move either backward or forward.

The game is over when one player has captured all of their opponent's pieces, or left their opponent with no more legal moves. When neither side can force a win, the game ends in a draw.

Coping with Data Structure Constraints

If you were to build this game using a high-level programming language like Java, Rust, Python, or even C++, then you would likely have a very different approach to setting up the data structures needed for the game than what you'll use in WebAssembly.

From the rules described in the previous section, you're going to need to hold the state of an 8×8 game board. The positions on this game board can be empty, or they can hold black or white pieces. In this section, you'll learn how to manage this kind of state in WebAssembly using nothing but the limited data structures available to the language.

If you're playing along with the home game, then you'll be creating functions throughout the chapter as you're exposed to more fundamental WebAssembly language primitives and concepts. To get started, let's create a directory for our project. I called mine wasmcheckers but you can choose anything. One advantage of writing code at this low level is we're just going to end up with a single text file—no project files, no Makefiles, just text.

Create a checkers.wat file in your project directory and define an empty module:

```
(module
  (memory $mem 1)
)
```

The 1 in the memory declaration indicates that the memory named $mem must have at least one 64KB page of memory allocated to it. Memory can grow at the request of either the Wasm module or the host.

You can compile this with wat2wasm and then examine the contents with wasm-objdump before moving on to the details of state management. You should see some output that looks like the following:

```
$ wasm-objdump checkers.wasm -x

checkers.wasm:  file format wasm 0x1

Section Details:

Memory:
 - memory[0] pages: initial=1
```

As you continue through this chapter, if you get curious about things you can always compile and then use the tools to examine what ended up in the compiled module.

Managing Game Board State

The first thing to tackle when it comes to managing the state of a game board is, obviously, the board itself. As mentioned, a checkerboard is an 8×8 grid. This probably triggers the part of your programmer brain that wants to declare a two-dimensional array. In Rust, that might look something like this:

```
let mut checkerboard: [[GamePiece; 8]; 8];
```

This is how most developers tend to visualize this problem, differences in syntax aside. But here's the rub: WebAssembly doesn't have arrays—single-dimension or otherwise. It also doesn't have complex types, so you can't create a struct or a tuple or even a hash map called GamePiece.

One thing that WebAssembly *does* have is *linear memory*. As we discussed in the preceding chapter, WebAssembly can have named, contiguous blocks of memory that it can write to, read from, import, or export. So if you're going to use a linear memory block, how do you represent a two-dimensional array in that space?

The solution is to linearize the two-dimensional array. Many of your favorite programming languages most likely already do this linearization for efficiency without you noticing. The trick to linearization is figuring out the math behind converting an (x,y) coordinate pair into a memory offset.

In this figure, you can see some blocks that represent values in individual positions in memory. Above some of these are the corresponding (x,y) coordinate on the game board and below you see the *unit offset* of that piece of memory. For example, the coordinate (0,0) on the board is at unit offset 0. The coordinate (7,0) on the game board is at unit offset 7, coordinate (7,1) is at unit offset 15, and so on:

You may have detected a pattern, and the equation for that pattern is offset = (x + y*8), where 8 is the number of squares in a row. This would be fine if you were just linearizing a two-dimensional array into a one-dimensional space indexed as an array, but WebAssembly's memory isn't indexed like an array. It's indexed by *byte*.

This means that if you're going to store a 32-bit integer (4 bytes) in each spot on the game board, you need to adjust the equation to offset = (x + y*8) * 4 where 4 is the number of bytes per unit offset.

Thinking about data storage this way activated a part of my brain I had long since thought dead and covered in cobwebs. It takes a little getting used to, and it may feel like a harsh constraint compared to what you're used to, but if you stick with this until the end of the chapter, you'll see how operating within these constraints pays off.

The foundation of the entire checkers game will be a function that determines the byte offset for a given X and Y coordinate, as this will be something your code is going to need to do every time it updates the board (this is inside the module declaration, after the memory declaration):

```
wasmcheckers/checkers.wat
(func $indexForPosition (param $x i32) (param $y i32) (result i32)
  (i32.add
    (i32.mul
      (i32.const 8)
      (get_local $y)
    )
    (get_local $x)
  )
)
;; Offset = ( x + y * 8 ) * 4
(func $offsetForPosition (param $x i32) (param $y i32) (result i32)
  (i32.mul
    (call $indexForPosition (get_local $x) (get_local $y))
    (i32.const 4)
  )
)
```

The math being performed here boils down to the following:

```
offsetForPosition(1, 2)
= (1 + 2 * 8) * 4
= 68
```

The nesting of the multiplication and addition operators is a little tough to read, but it's still manageable. Armed with the ability to determine where to put your game state, the next step is to figure out how to represent that state.

Fun with Bit Flags

In each of the locations in linear memory, you have access to 32 bits (or 4 bytes). You don't have the luxury of a complex structure or any language primitives for storing lists, fields, or tuples. You've just got raw bits, so how are you going to represent game state?

This dusts off another technique from the patterns vault called *bit flags*. Bit flags is a technique for assigning meaning to individual bits within a number. When more than one consecutive bit are combined to store some other meaning, that's typically called *bit masking*. Most of what we're going to do is bit flags, though we'll touch on masking briefly.

You can see the 8-bit number 00101101, but rather than simply meaning the numerical constant 45, this is actually a set of boolean values. As the previous image indicates, the value 45 carries all of the following meaning within the context of a fictional video game:

- This game object is a player
- Game object is *not* illuminated
- Tutorial is completed
- Healer has been discovered
- The Elven king has not been slain
- The player has access to fire magic
- The player has not yet unlocked the cave of nightmares
- The player is not a game master

When you describe certain data structures this way, you end up passing around simple, raw numeric values to represent players and game objects rather than high-level constructs like structs or enums.

Given strategies like bit flags or masking, it's kind of surprising just how much information you can pack into a single number. Underneath all of your higher level languages, many structs are getting densely packed into numbers just like this. Tooling and compilers doing all this work on your behalf is a recurring theme, and you're looking at the individual gears within your familiar machine now.

You can use *bitwise* logical operators on numbers to query and manipulate these bit values. For example, a bitwise AND operation compares each bit of one number with the corresponding bit of a second number, and if both bits in the same relative position are 1, then the bit in the resulting number will be 1. Otherwise, the output bit will be 0. A bitwise OR produces a 1 when either of the two compared bits are 1, and a bitwise XOR performs an exclusive or on the compared bits.

The following quick reference table will come in super handy when working with bit masked or "packed" values:

Logical Operation	WebAssembly	Bitmask Action
AND	i32.and	Query the value of a bit
OR	i32.or	Sets a bit to true (1)
XOR	i32.xor	Toggles the value of a bit

So far, you've written a function that lets you convert a Cartesian checkerboard coordinate into a memory address, and you've seen how you can pack lots of data into simple integers for storage and retrieval. Now you can assign meaning to the bits of an integer on a checkerboard:

Binary Value	Decimal Value	Game Meaning
[unused 24 bits]...00000000	0	Unoccupied Square
[unused 24 bits]...00000001	1	Black Piece
[unused 24 bits]...00000010	2	White Piece
[unused 24 bits]...00000100	4	Crowned Piece

Using these bit flags, you know that a crowned black piece will have a value of 5 (crowned + black), a crowned white piece will have a value of 6 (crowned + white), and all empty spaces on the board will be represented by 0s. If you have a keen eye, you may have noticed that this bit-packed data structure technically allows for a piece to be both white and black at the same time (a value of 3). Keeping the piece colors mutually exclusive will have to be something you enforce with code, though you could also use different bit flag meanings to avoid this situation if you wanted.

Bitwise versus Regular Math

You might have noticed that to activate multiple boolean flags within a bit masked value, you can simply add the two flags together, as in the case of Black (1) and Crowned (4) equals 5. This is a bad idea because this operation isn't *idempotent*. If you add the Crown flag to a number twice, you've basically corrupted your state. When you activate a flag with i32.or, that's idempotent, and you can do it over and over again without corrupting the rest of the number.

Once you decide what each bit means, you can write some functions to query, set, and remove these values from a piece. And in this case, a "piece" is literally nothing more than a 4-byte integer value:

```
wasmcheckers/checkers.wat
;; Determine if a piece has been crowned
(func $isCrowned (param $piece i32) (result i32)
  (i32.eq
    (i32.and (get_local $piece) (get_global $CROWN))
    (get_global $CROWN)
  )
)

;; Determine if a piece is white
(func $isWhite (param $piece i32) (result i32)
  (i32.eq
    (i32.and (get_local $piece) (get_global $WHITE))
    (get_global $WHITE)
  )
)

;; Determine if a piece is black
(func $isBlack (param $piece i32) (result i32)
  (i32.eq
    (i32.and (get_local $piece) (get_global $BLACK))
    (get_global $BLACK)
  )
)

;; Adds a crown to a given piece (no mutation)
(func $withCrown (param $piece i32) (result i32)
  (i32.or (get_local $piece) (get_global $CROWN))
)

;; Removes a crown from a given piece (no mutation)
(func $withoutCrown (param $piece i32) (result i32)
 (i32.and (get_local $piece) (i32.const 3))
)
```

This code relies on immutable global values like $CROWN, $BLACK, and $WHITE that act like constants would in other languages. These are defined at the top of the module like so:

```
(global $WHITE  i32 (i32.const 2))
(global $BLACK  i32 (i32.const 1))
(global $CROWN  i32 (i32.const 4))
```

The withoutCrown function is a bit tricky. We can't use XOR with the crown bit (4) to force it to be zero. That will instead *toggle* it, setting the bit for a piece that isn't already crowned. The intent of this function is to compare two pieces regardless of their crown status. The safe way to do this is to use AND with a mask that only returns the black and white bits and ignores all else.

For me, as someone who doesn't think in binary and bitwise operations all day, this was difficult to visualize. Take a look at the following truth table that illustrates how this works:

Value	Meaning	Operation	Mask	Result
0101	Crowned Black	&	0011	0001 (B)
0001	Uncrowned Black	&	0011	0001 (B)
0110	Crowned White	&	0011	0010 (W)

$withCrown works on the same bitmasking principal, just with a different operator. This code invokes i32.or on the bits in the $piece variable and the bits in the 32-bit constant 4. Referring to our handy bitmasking reference chart, we know that the OR bitwise operation is used to *set* a bit. So, the bit in the third spot from the right (2^2) will be set to 1 and the new value is returned.

It's important to remember here that you're not (yet) affecting stored state, you're just playing with the bits inside numbers. At this point you've created some functions that perform bit masking operations on simple integers to give them contextual meaning within the checkers game.

Before we move on to writing more code, it would be nice to be able to test and experiment with the functions we're writing. Since you're using raw wast syntax, there's no easy unit testing framework or code generation available. The easiest thing to do is just export all the functions we're working on so we can invoke them from JavaScript until we're satisfied they work as intended. First, put $offsetForPosition, $indexForPosition, and all of the bitmasking functions into a test module called func_test.wat:

```
wasmcheckers/func_test.wat
(module
  (memory $mem 1)
  (global $WHITE  i32 (i32.const 2))
  (global $BLACK  i32 (i32.const 1))
  (global $CROWN  i32 (i32.const 4))

(func $indexForPosition (param $x i32) (param $y i32) (result i32)
  (i32.add
    (i32.mul
      (i32.const 8)
      (get_local $y)
    )
    (get_local $x)
  )
)
)
```

```
;; Offset = ( x + y * 8 ) * 4
(func $offsetForPosition (param $x i32) (param $y i32) (result i32)
  (i32.mul
    (call $indexForPosition (get_local $x) (get_local $y))
    (i32.const 4)
  )
)

;; Determine if a piece has been crowned
(func $isCrowned (param $piece i32) (result i32)
  (i32.eq
    (i32.and (get_local $piece) (get_global $CROWN))
    (get_global $CROWN)
  )
)

;; Determine if a piece is white
(func $isWhite (param $piece i32) (result i32)
  (i32.eq
    (i32.and (get_local $piece) (get_global $WHITE))
    (get_global $WHITE)
  )
)

;; Determine if a piece is black
(func $isBlack (param $piece i32) (result i32)
  (i32.eq
    (i32.and (get_local $piece) (get_global $BLACK))
    (get_global $BLACK)
  )
)

;; Adds a crown to a given piece (no mutation)
(func $withCrown (param $piece i32) (result i32)
  (i32.or (get_local $piece) (get_global $CROWN))
)

;; Removes a crown from a given piece (no mutation)
(func $withoutCrown (param $piece i32) (result i32)
 (i32.and (get_local $piece) (i32.const 3))
)

  (export "offsetForPosition" (func $offsetForPosition))
  (export "isCrowned" (func $isCrowned))
  (export "isWhite" (func $isWhite))
  (export "isBlack" (func $isBlack))
  (export "withCrown" (func $withCrown))
  (export "withoutCrown" (func $withoutCrown))
)
```

Compile that into func_test.wasm with wat2wasm, then create a JavaScript wrapper that will load the WebAssembly module and execute the exported functions so we can make sure they're working as we expect:

wasmcheckers/func_test.js

```
fetch('./func_test.wasm').then(response =>
  response.arrayBuffer()
).then(bytes => WebAssembly.instantiate(bytes)).then(results => {
  console.log("Loaded wasm module");
  instance = results.instance;
  console.log("instance", instance);

  var white = 2;
  var black = 1;
  var crowned_white = 6;
  var crowned_black = 5;

  console.log("Calling offset");
  var offset = instance.exports.offsetForPosition(3,4);
  console.log("Offset for 3,4 is ",offset);

  console.debug("White is white?", instance.exports.isWhite(white));
  console.debug("Black is black?", instance.exports.isBlack(black));
  console.debug("Black is white?", instance.exports.isWhite(black));
  console.debug("Uncrowned white",
    instance.exports.isWhite(instance.exports.withoutCrown(crowned_white)));
  console.debug("Uncrowned black",
    instance.exports.isBlack(instance.exports.withoutCrown(crowned_black)));
  console.debug("Crowned is crowned",
    instance.exports.isCrowned(crowned_black));
  console.debug("Crowned is crowned (b)",
    instance.exports.isCrowned(crowned_white));
});
```

Finally, we can create a little index.html file that starts the func_test.js script:

wasmcheckers/func_test.html

```
<!DOCTYPE html>
<html>

<head>
  <meta charset="utf-8">
  <style>
    body {
      background-color: rgb(255, 255, 255);
    }
  </style>
</head>

<body>
  <span id="container"></span>
  <script src="./func_test.js"></script>
</body>

</html>
```

Because of cross-site scripting rules in the browser, it might not let you open a file from the file system without having an HTTP server (my Firefox on

Ubuntu won't, but apparently Firefox on Arch Linux does), so spin up your favorite one or you can just use Python to launch this lightweight one in the same directory as your HTML file:

```
$ python3 -m http.server
Serving HTTP on 0.0.0.0 port 8000 (http://0.0.0.0:8000/) ...
```

Now open your browser to localhost:8000/func_test.html. Open up the JavaScript debug console and you should see something like the following output, verifying that we're getting the values we expect:

```
Loaded wasm module
instance WebAssembly.Instance { exports: {…} }
Calling offset
Offset for 3,4 is   140
White is white 1
Black is black 1
Black is not white 0
Uncrowned white 1
Uncrowned black 1
Crowned is crowned 1
Crowned is crowned (b) 1
```

While reassuring (our code works), this is also a boring and dry set of console output. As we progress further in the book, you'll be able to produce real, user-facing web visualizations of state, game boards, and other module internals.

As you progress through this chapter, you can just copy and paste whatever function you like into this harness, make sure it's exported, and test it with JavaScript. In the next section, you'll build on what you've coded in checkers.wat so far to start reading and writing game state to manage the checkerboard.

Manipulating the Board

The next couple of functions you're going to write involve storing and retrieving values from the game board grid in linear memory and performing some validation checks on parameters and data before allowing state mutation:

```
wasmcheckers/checkers.wat
;; Sets a piece on the board.
(func $setPiece (param $x i32) (param $y i32) (param $piece i32)
  (i32.store
    (call $offsetForPosition
      (get_local $x)
      (get_local $y)
    )
    (get_local $piece)
  )
)
```

```
;; Gets a piece from the board. Out of range causes a trap
(func $getPiece (param $x i32) (param $y i32) (result i32)
  (if (result i32)
    (block (result i32)
      (i32.and
        (call $inRange
          (i32.const 0)
          (i32.const 7)
          (get_local $x)
        )
        (call $inRange
          (i32.const 0)
          (i32.const 7)
          (get_local $y)
        )
      )
    )
    (then
      (i32.load
        (call $offsetForPosition
          (get_local $x)
          (get_local $y))
      )
    )
    (else
      (unreachable)
    )
  )
)

;; Detect if values are within range (inclusive high and low)
(func $inRange (param $low i32) (param $high i32)
              (param $value i32) (result i32)
  (i32.and
    (i32.ge_s (get_local $value) (get_local $low))
    (i32.le_s (get_local $value) (get_local $high))
  )
)
```

The $setPiece function has some new syntax, and this is the first place where your code uses the return value from one function as a parameter to another function. $setPiece calls i32.store, which stores a 32-bit integer in a memory address. The memory address will be the value returned by calling $offsetForPosition, and the value stored will be the parameter $piece. For example, to set a white piece at grid position (5,5), you could call (i32.store 200 2).

$getPiece illustrates the first use of an if block with a function call as a predicate. You need to specify the type of the value that'll be returned from a predicate if it executes a function. The block keyword simply wraps one or more statements and indicates the return type of that block, kind of like an anonymous function. The general structure for an if/then/else block that also executes code in the predicate clause looks like this:

```
(if (result i32) (block (result i32) ...)
    (then ... )
    (else ... )
)
```

Finally, the $inRange function is used to prevent querying beyond the edge of the game board. Most high-level programming languages have built-in features that will prevent situations like this or will throw an out-of-bounds runtime exception. Without those luxuries, in WebAssembly you've got to manually ensure you never access memory beyond the bounds of a given data structure.

It's worth pointing out, however, that even an index out-of-bounds error in WebAssembly can never reach beyond the limits of its linear memory. This keeps the chance of heap corruption pretty low.

Bounds Checking Blunders

Throughout computing history, failing to properly check bounds at the assembly level has resulted in some catastrophic bugs, malicious viruses, and some amazing video game exploits. One of my favorites is this one from the original Famicom version of *The Legend of Zelda*,[a] which shows how reading beyond implied bounds can convert raw data into executable instructions to teleport straight to the end of the game.

---

a.   youtu.be/fj9u00PMkYU

Keeping Track of the Current Turn

The game board itself isn't the only bit of state that needs to be maintained in a checkers game. You'll need to keep track of who has the next move. For obvious reasons, the checkers engine needs to prevent a player from taking two turns in a row or moving pieces that don't belong to them.

You've already defined two different values to indicate piece color: 1 for black and 2 for white. In a regular programming language you might simply create a global variable called currentTurn and set that to an enum like White or Black. With WebAssembly, we can create global variables that are either private to the module or can be shared with the host. Let's take a look at the global declaration near the top of the module:

```
(memory $mem 1)
(global $currentTurn (mut i32) (i32.const 0))
```

When we declare global variables in wast (raw text WebAssembly syntax), we can specify their mutability (immutable globals can be treated like constants in other languages), and we need to specify an initial value. The $currentTurn global will be set to 1 when it is black's turn and 2 when it is white's turn. The following code is responsible for querying and updating the current turn state:

wasmcheckers/checkers.wat

```
;; Gets the current turn owner (white or black)
(func $getTurnOwner (result i32)
    (get_global $currentTurn)
)

;; At the end of a turn, switch turn owner to the other player
(func $toggleTurnOwner
  (if (i32.eq (call $getTurnOwner) (i32.const 1))
    (then (call $setTurnOwner (i32.const 2)))
    (else (call $setTurnOwner (i32.const 1)))
  )
)

;; Sets the turn owner
(func $setTurnOwner (param $piece i32)
  (set_global $currentTurn (get_local $piece))
)

;; Determine if it's a player's turn
(func $isPlayersTurn (param $player i32) (result i32)
  (i32.gt_s
    (i32.and (get_local $player) (call $getTurnOwner))
    (i32.const 0)
  )
)
```

To check whether it is a current player's turn, we might be tempted to check if the value of $player is the same as the value returned by $isPlayersTurn. The problem is that $player can be holding a value indicating a crowned piece, which would mess up our equality check.

To compensate for this, when the $isPlayersTurn function checks if the player value passed is the current player, it will perform an *AND* (remember, this queries *only* the bits in the mask) of the value and the player, and if that is greater than zero, that player is the color currently stored in the $currentTurn global. This is kind of like comparing player.color with currenturn.color in other, higher-level programming languages. Here, think of the concept of "color" as a bitmask.

Implementing Game Rules

From a rules standpoint, checkers is not all that complex of a game. All 12 of your pieces start out with the same movement capabilities, and the only special pieces ever on the board are those that have been crowned.

The goal of this chapter isn't to produce a game of checkers that might be ready to plug into a WebGL site so you can ship it tomorrow. You're building a foundation for such a thing, but the nitty-gritty details of checkers edge-case rules are beyond the scope of this chapter.

This checkers game implements some basic rules like crowning a piece and moving. It doesn't implement jumps, multi-jumps, or detect a winner. If you would like to do that as a reader exercise, I would love to see your game on GitHub!

The first function in the following code listing, $shouldCrown, determines if a piece should be crowned. A piece is eligible for upgrade if it resides in its opponent's kings row. The $crownPiece function uses a few functions you've already written to add a crown to a piece and then store it in the gameboard:

wasmcheckers/checkers.wat
```
;; Should this piece get crowned?
;; We crown black pieces in row 0, white pieces in row 7
(func $shouldCrown (param $pieceY i32) (param $piece i32) (result i32)
  (i32.or
    (i32.and
      (i32.eq
        (get_local $pieceY)
        (i32.const 0)
      )
      (call $isBlack (get_local $piece))
    )
    (i32.and
      (i32.eq
        (get_local $pieceY)
        (i32.const 7)
      )
      (call $isWhite (get_local $piece))
    )
  )
)

;; Converts a piece into a crowned piece and invokes
;; a host notifier
(func $crownPiece (param $x i32) (param $y i32)
  (local $piece i32)
  (set_local $piece (call $getPiece (get_local $x)(get_local $y)))
```

```
  (call $setPiece (get_local $x) (get_local $y)
    (call $withCrown (get_local $piece)))

  (call $notify_piececrowned (get_local $x)(get_local $y))
)

(func $distance (param $x i32)(param $y i32)(result i32)
  (i32.sub (get_local $x) (get_local $y))
)
```

The local keyword declares a temporary variable that will only be visible within its enclosing scope. In the case of this code listing, all the locals are scoped to their containing function. The set_local instruction sets the value of a local variable. Sadly, you can't declare and set a local in the same line of code. High-level languages that allow this sort of thing are just generating the separate declaration and assignment operations on your behalf.

Another thing worth pointing out in the preceding code listing is the call to $notify_piececrowned. This function will be imported by this checkers module and implemented by the host. Whenever a piece is crowned, the module calls this to let the host react to the change. This could include modifying the sprite on display for the newly crowned piece, playing a victorious sound, or both.

The $distance function is just a simple subtraction. In the next section on movement, you'll see how that value is used to determine if that distance is valid.

Nearly all of the (naive) fundamentals of checkers are done at this point: the only thing left is to code player movement.

Moving Players

Before a player can move, you need to ensure that it is a valid move. In the case of this naive implementation of checkers, a valid move is:

- The "move distance" from current to target (single axis) is valid
- The target space is unoccupied
- The piece being moved belongs to the current player

Let's take a look at the code to determine if a move is valid:

wasmcheckers/checkers.wat
```
;; Determine if the move is valid
(func $isValidMove (param $fromX i32) (param $fromY i32)
                   (param $toX i32) (param $toY i32) (result i32)
  (local $player i32)
  (local $target i32)

  (set_local $player (call $getPiece (get_local $fromX) (get_local $fromY)))
  (set_local $target (call $getPiece (get_local $toX) (get_local $toY)))
```

```
      (if (result i32)
        (block (result i32)
          (i32.and
            (call $validJumpDistance (get_local $fromY) (get_local $toY))
            (i32.and
              (call $isPlayersTurn (get_local $player))
              ;; target must be unoccupied
              (i32.eq (get_local $target) (i32.const 0))
            )
          )
        )
        (then
          (i32.const 1)
        )
        (else
          (i32.const 0)
        )
      )
)

;; Ensures travel is 1 or 2 squares
(func $validJumpDistance (param $from i32) (param $to i32) (result i32)
  (local $d i32)
  (set_local $d
  (if (result i32)
    (i32.gt_s (get_local $to) (get_local $from))
    (then
      (call $distance (get_local $to) (get_local $from))
    )
    (else
      (call $distance (get_local $from) (get_local $to))
    ))
  )
  (i32.le_u
    (get_local $d)
    (i32.const 2)
  )
)
```

The code for $validJumpDistance might look a little strange. Since WebAssembly's integers don't support the abs() function, we're basically deciding on the order in which we supply arguments to the $distance function based on whether or not it will result in a negative number. Also remember that we're not building a rules-compliant version of checkers—this is *just enough* code to exercise some basic rules in service of learning WebAssembly.

In the following code listing, the $move function will eventually be exported (typically done at the end of the module code) function so the host can call it. Since this makes it a public API method, it has to guard against bad data and invalid moves. $move returns 1 for a successful move and 0 for a failed one:

```
wasmcheckers/checkers.wat
;; Exported move function to be called by the game host
(func $move (param $fromX i32) (param $fromY i32)
            (param $toX i32) (param $toY i32) (result i32)
  (if (result i32)
    (block (result i32)
      (call $isValidMove (get_local $fromX) (get_local $fromY)
                         (get_local $toX) (get_local $toY))
    )
    (then
      (call $do_move (get_local $fromX) (get_local $fromY)
                     (get_local $toX) (get_local $toY))
    )
    (else
      (i32.const 0)
    )
  )
)
```

Notice that the $move function defers some functionality to the $do_move function. This separates the conditional guard checking code from the actual state changes in $do_move. After a move toggles the current turn owner, the state change sets the piece at the destination location, and wipes out the piece at the original location:

```
wasmcheckers/checkers.wat
;; Internal move function, performs actual move post-validation of target.
;; Currently not handled:
;;    - removing opponent piece during a jump
;;    - detecting win condition
(func $do_move (param $fromX i32) (param $fromY i32)
               (param $toX i32) (param $toY i32) (result i32)
  (local $curpiece i32)
  (set_local $curpiece (call $getPiece (get_local $fromX)(get_local $fromY)))

  (call $toggleTurnOwner)
  (call $setPiece (get_local $toX) (get_local $toY) (get_local $curpiece))
  (call $setPiece (get_local $fromX) (get_local $fromY) (i32.const 0))
  (if (call $shouldCrown (get_local $toY) (get_local $curpiece))
    (then (call $crownPiece (get_local $toX) (get_local $toY))))
  (call $notify_piecemoved (get_local $fromX) (get_local $fromY)
                           (get_local $toX) (get_local $toY))
  (i32.const 1)
)
```

As a convenience, the $do_move function invokes a function called $notify_piece-moved that lets the host know when a piece has finished moving. This function will be declared as an import at the beginning of the module. This function is called so the host can react to player movement rather than repeatedly polling for changes to the game board state.

Finally, with all the basic functions in place, it's time to connect this module to a host and test it.

Testing Wasm Checkers

Before you can start testing or playing checkers, you need just one more function. You've written functions to maintain the game board state, to move player pieces, and even to notify the host when important events occur. What's missing is the initial set up—placing all of the players' pieces on the board.

$initBoard is a simple, brute-force function that just calls $setPiece over and over to place the white and black pieces, finally setting the current turn to black:

```
;; Manually place each piece on the board to initialize the game
(func $initBoard
  ;; Place the white pieces at the top of the board
  (call $setPiece (i32.const 1) (i32.const 0) (i32.const 2))
  (call $setPiece (i32.const 3) (i32.const 0) (i32.const 2))
  (call $setPiece (i32.const 5) (i32.const 0) (i32.const 2))
  (call $setPiece (i32.const 7) (i32.const 0) (i32.const 2))

  «many, many more calls to $setPiece»

  (call $setTurnOwner (i32.const 1)) ;; Black goes first
)
```

The next step is to include all the imports at the top of the checkers.wat module:

wasmcheckers/checkers.wat
```
(import "events" "piecemoved"
       (func $notify_piecemoved (param $fromX i32) (param $fromY i32)
                                (param $toX i32) (param $toY i32)))
(import "events" "piececrowned"
       (func $notify_piececrowned (param $pieceX i32) (param $pieceY i32)))
```

And declare the exports at the bottom of the module:

wasmcheckers/checkers.wat
```
(export "getPiece" (func $getPiece))
(export "isCrowned" (func $isCrowned))
(export "initBoard" (func $initBoard))
(export "getTurnOwner" (func $getTurnOwner))
(export "move" (func $move))
(export "memory" (memory $mem))
```

It is important to notice that not all of the functions are exported. The host is limited to invoking only the public (exported) API. For example, you do not export $setPiece, which could possibly let the host code cheat or allow a bug to corrupt the game board. This is a standard defensive programming practice.

With the checkers.wat file complete, you should be able to build it using wat2wasm:

```
$ /path/to/wabt/bin/wat2wasm checkers.wat -o checkers.wasm
```

Next, create an index.js file to load the module and run through some sample moves:

```
wasmcheckers/index.js
fetch('./checkers.wasm').then(response =>
  response.arrayBuffer()
).then(bytes => WebAssembly.instantiate(bytes, {
  events: {
    piecemoved: (fX, fY, tX, tY) => {
      console.log("A piece moved from (" + fX + "," + fY +
        ") to (" + tX + "," + tY + ")");
    },
    piececrowned: (x, y) => {
      console.log("A piece was crowned at (" + x + "," + y + ")");
    }
  },
}
)).then(results => {
  instance = results.instance;

  instance.exports.initBoard();
  console.log("At start, turn owner is " +
    instance.exports.getTurnOwner());

  instance.exports.move(0, 5, 0, 4); // B
  instance.exports.move(1, 0, 1, 1); // W
  instance.exports.move(0, 4, 0, 3); // B
  instance.exports.move(1, 1, 1, 0); // W
  instance.exports.move(0, 3, 0, 2); // B
  instance.exports.move(1, 0, 1, 1); // W
  instance.exports.move(0, 2, 0, 0); // B - this will get a crown
  instance.exports.move(1, 1, 1, 0); // W
  // B - move the crowned piece out
  let res = instance.exports.move(0, 0, 0, 2);

  document.getElementById("container").innerText = res;
  console.log("At end, turn owner is " + instance.exports.getTurnOwner());
}).catch(console.error);
```

The moves in this test are just exercising the naive game rules. A real game wouldn't allow movement like this, but this at least helps us verify that the code we did write works as intended. Now you can create an index.html file that will run this script:

```
wasmcheckers/index.html
<!DOCTYPE html>
<html>

<head>
  <meta charset="utf-8">
  <style>
    body {
      background-color: rgb(255, 255, 255);
    }
  </style>
</head>

<body>
  <span id="container"></span>
  <script src="./index.js"></script>
</body>

</html>
```

As you did earlier in the chapter, you can host this file behind a simple Python web server:

```
$ python3 -m http.server
Serving HTTP on 0.0.0.0 port 8000 (http://0.0.0.0:8000/) ...
```

You should now be able to point your browser at localhost:8000, open the developer tools, and see the following in your JavaScript console:

```
At start, turn owner is 1
A piece moved from (0,5) to (0,4)
A piece moved from (1,0) to (1,1)
A piece moved from (0,4) to (0,3)
A piece moved from (1,1) to (1,0)
A piece moved from (0,3) to (0,2)
A piece moved from (1,0) to (1,1)
A piece was crowned at (0,0)
A piece moved from (0,2) to (0,0)
A piece moved from (1,1) to (1,0)
A piece moved from (0,0) to (0,2)
```

The module works, so we've got that going for us. Take a step back and bask in the glow of knowing that you've written WebAssembly to handle in-memory game board state, turn management, game rule validation, and even notify the host when important events occur. Before you rush off to make millions on your new checkers game, there's one more thing you *really* need to see—take a look at the file size of your compiled wasm module:

```
$ ls -l
total 48
-rw-r--r-- 1 kevin kevin  853 Oct 28 13:08 checkers.wasm
-rw-r--r-- 1 kevin kevin 9952 Oct 28 11:04 checkers.wat
-rw-r--r-- 1 kevin kevin  243 Oct 28 10:38 func_test.html
-rw-r--r-- 1 kevin kevin 1063 Oct 28 11:13 func_test.js
-rw-r--r-- 1 kevin kevin  184 Oct 28 10:57 func_test.wasm
-rw-r--r-- 1 kevin kevin 1405 Oct 28 10:57 func_test.wat
-rw-r--r-- 1 kevin kevin  238 Jul  7 15:16 index.html
-rw-r--r-- 1 kevin kevin 1072 Jul 15 10:57 index.js
```

Your eyes are not deceiving you—the compiled size of the checkers module is a mere *853* bytes! It might vary a bit depending on your OS and file system, but it will still be *tiny*. You also know, because you wrote all your own state management code, that the checkers module will never use more than a single 64KB page of memory. In fact, your module only uses a grand total of 256 bytes of linear memory. Just think about how many simultaneous, in-memory copies of a live checkers game a server could hold.

You'll see in subsequent chapters that as you add tooling and code generation, this will dramatically affect the size of your wasm modules. Some of the tools you've seen so far can also be used to trim out some of the excess fat from these modules, but you'll never be able to create modules this small unless you're hand-coding your wat.

Wrapping Up

There was more to this chapter than just learning how to write WebAssembly "the hard way." Even now, in the early days of the WebAssembly ecosystem, multiple layers of tooling and code generation are available that can easily hide the inner workings from you.

Because you've written more than just a simple module that adds two numbers together, you know what's going on at the bottom levels of abstraction. More importantly, you can *appreciate* what tools and code generators will do for you. This gives you a deeper understanding of the consequences of the Rust code you'll write and the design decisions you'll make when building WebAssembly solutions. Further, when you get to the chapter on hosting WebAssembly with Rust, you will already have an in-depth knowledge of the components of a WebAssembly module and so the parsing, loading, and executing tasks will all make more sense.

In the next chapter, you'll start to write at higher levels of abstraction, using Rust to target WebAssembly. As you explore that chapter, keep in mind what you've learned so far, as keeping a mental map between high-level code and its raw WebAssembly equivalent will help you squeeze every ounce of power, performance, and elegance from WebAssembly.

Part II

Interacting with JavaScript

In this part, we'll expand on our foundation by learning how to build WebAssembly modules with Rust and integrate them with JavaScript and the browser.

CHAPTER 3

Wading into WebAssembly with Rust

The first part of this book introduced you to the world of WebAssembly. You learned about its internals and its architecture, what stack machines are, and where WebAssembly fits within the larger world of web applications. You even built a mostly functioning checkers module entirely in wast, the text representation of WebAssembly instructions.

In this part of the book, you will focus not only on increasing your ability to interweave WebAssembly and JavaScript functionality, but you will also go through an introduction to Rust and you will see how you can use it to add strong types, memory safety, and elegant, expressive code to your WebAssembly modules.

In this chapter, you'll get an introduction to Rust and get your workstation tooling set up to target WebAssembly from Rust. By the end of this chapter, you'll build a new version of the checkers module entirely in Rust. The Rust language has a longer learning curve than other languages like Go. As such, you might want to start skimming through the official Rust book[1] to get familiar with some of the syntax coming up in the book. It's not required, but consulting multiple reference sources is never a bad idea.

Introducing Rust

If you're already well versed in Rust, then feel free to skip to the next section. If you're new to it or you'd like a refresher on the core concepts of the language, then you may find this section beneficial.

Rust started in 2006 as Graydon Hoare's personal project while he was working for Mozilla. Mozilla sponsored it in 2009 and announced it in 2010. In the history of each programming language, its *genesis moment* is when a

---

1.   doc.rust-lang.org/book/

compiler written in that language is able to compile that language—a compiler inception,[2] if you will. For Rust, this came in 2011 and the first stable 1.0 release came in 2015.

Rust has been gaining in popularity exponentially ever since. In addition to powering Mozilla's new browser layout engine and showing up in a number of high-visibility systems and networking open source projects, it won the "Most Loved Programming Language" award in 2016, 2017, and 2018,[3] surpassing Kotlin, Python, TypeScript, and even Go. This is Rust's elevator pitch from the official website:

> Rust is a systems programming language that runs blazingly fast, prevents segfaults, and guarantees thread safety.

Some of the main characteristics of the Rust language that make it appealing for building applications with WebAssembly include:

Safety

Rust doesn't have the concept of null. Instead, any data that can be missing is represented as an Option type. This gets rid of an entire class of errors that plagues other systems languages like C and C++ and even many higher-level languages. In addition to lack of nulls, Rust will prevent your code from compiling if it could potentially create a data race, free already deallocated resources, or access something that has gone out of scope.

Expressivity

Despite being labeled as a "systems language," Rust has a remarkably expressive syntax and includes many features that people typically laud when talking about functional programming: pattern matching, destructuring, streams, iterators, and much more. Combined with the concepts of traits and generics, Rust (most of the time) manages to facilitate highly readable and maintainable code.

Performance

Rust binaries are standalone, native binaries. They consume relatively little disk space, have a fairly small memory footprint, and the code generally performs extremely well. Despite all of the additional safety constraints in the language, Rust doesn't need a garbage collector, which can often produce raw, C-like performance.

---

2. en.wikipedia.org/wiki/Bootstrapping_(compilers)
3. insights.stackoverflow.com/survey/2018/#most-loved-dreaded-and-wanted

Installing Rust

It's time to start writing some Rust. The first thing you'll need to do is follow the installation instructions from the official Rust[4] website. On that site, you'll find a curl script you can run that will install rustup, the main entry point into the Rust toolchain.

Once you've completed the installation appropriate for your system, you should be able to interrogate the version of the Rust compiler:

```
$ rustc --version
rustc 1.30.1 (1433507eb 2018-11-07)
```

Rust is on a six-week release cycle for the stable toolchain, so your version will very likely be newer than the one in this book. You need to be able to successfully run rustc and rustup before continuing to the next section.

Building Hello WebAssembly in Rust

Rust's tools intrinsically support the notion of multiple targets. You can compile for different targets without having to run the compilation on that target machine. For example, you can target an ARM architecture (e.g., Raspberry Pi) from a regular workstation.

WebAssembly manifests as a target in Rust's toolchain. In addition to the regular six-week releases, Rust also has a nightly build that enables newer language features that haven't yet stabilized. As of Rust version 1.30, most of the WebAssembly tools and libraries you'll encounter in this book should build just fine on the stable toolchain.

Installing the WebAssembly Target

If you issue the command, rustup toolchain list, you'll see a toolchain that looks something like stable-x86_64-unknown-linux-gnu (default) (this will vary by operating system). Next, you can add the WebAssembly target by typing rustup target add wasm32-unknown-unknown. This may also take some time and will get everything set up for that target. If you're curious about all of the targets Rust supports, you can type rustup target list. This list also shows which targets are installed and which one is the default.

---

4. www.rust-lang.org/en-US/install.html

Creating a WebAssembly Project

You can use *Cargo*, Rust's project build tool, to create new empty projects. To create one for your first WebAssembly project, type the following:

```
$ cargo new --lib rustwasmhello
Created library `rustwasmhello` project
```

This creates a Cargo.toml file in the rustwasmhello directory. Edit this file so that it looks like this:

```
rustwasmhello/Cargo.toml
[package]
name = "rustwasmhello"
version = "0.1.0"
authors = ["Your Name <your.email@address.com>"]

[lib]
crate-type = ["cdylib"]

[dependencies]
```

The only lines in this file that differ from what you get by default from cargo is the indicator that this project will expose a C-style dynamic library, which is then used by other linkers to produce a WebAssembly module:

```
[lib]
crate-type = ["cdylib"]
```

Now edit the lib.rs file that cargo created and set its contents to the following:

```
rustwasmhello/src/lib.rs
#[no_mangle]
pub extern "C" fn add_one(x: i32) -> i32 {
    x + 1
}
```

This code should look familiar. It's the same code that you saw in the first chapter when you created a WebAssembly Studio project online. This project should now be ready to compile into a WebAssembly module. The first step is to tell cargo to build it (make sure you're in the rustwasmhello directory):

```
$ cargo build --target wasm32-unknown-unknown
Compiling rustwasmhello v0.1.0
    (file:///home/kevin/Code/Rust/wasmbook_text/khrust/Book/code/rustwasmhello)
Finished dev [unoptimized + debuginfo] target(s) in 0.24s
```

This produced a rustwasmhello.wasm file under the target/wasm32-unknown-unknown/debug folder. To see that your release build will produce a Wasm file very similar to something that you'd get building it by hand, first compile in release mode:

```
$ cargo build --release --target=wasm32-unknown-unknown
   Compiling rustwasmhello v0.1.0
     (/home/kevin/Code/Rust/wasmbook/khrust/Book/code/rustwasmhello)
Finished release [optimized] target(s) in 0.12s
```

Now you can verify that the output contains an exported function called add_one by using the wasm-objdump tool:

```
$ wasm-objdump -x target/wasm32-unknown-unknown/release/rustwasmhello.wasm

rustwasmhello.wasm:      file format wasm 0x1

Section Details:

Type:
 - type[0] () -> nil
 - type[1] (i32) -> i32
Function:
 - func[0] sig=0 <__wasm_call_ctors>
 - func[1] sig=1 <add_one>
Table:
 - table[0] type=anyfunc initial=1 max=1
Memory:
 - memory[0] pages: initial=16
Global:
 - global[0] i32 mutable=1 - init i32=1048576
 - global[1] i32 mutable=0 - init i32=1048576
 - global[2] i32 mutable=0 - init i32=1048576
Export:
 - memory[0] -> "memory"
 - table[0] -> "__indirect_function_table"
 - global[1] -> "__heap_base"
 - global[2] -> "__data_end"
 - func[1] <add_one> -> "add_one"
Custom:
 - name: ".debug_info"
Custom:
 - name: ".debug_macinfo"
Custom:
 - name: ".debug_pubtypes"
Custom:
 - name: ".debug_ranges"
Custom:
 - name: ".debug_abbrev"
Custom:
 - name: ".debug_line"
Custom:
 - name: ".debug_str"
Custom:
 - name: ".debug_pubnames"
```

```
Custom:
  - name: "name"
  - func[0] <__wasm_call_ctors>
  - func[1] <add_one>
```

You can see that this module comes with a single function table, a default 16-page (16 * 64KB) block of linear memory, some globals, and the add_one() function that we wrote.

Congratulations, you've compiled your first Rust WebAssembly module. Now it's time to learn some cool Rust features while you build out a new checkers module.

Creating Rusty Checkers

This section has a very specific goal: build a new checkers module entirely in Rust WebAssembly that conforms as closely as possible to the interface of the hand-written one from the previous chapter.

Diving into Rust is no small feat, so to keep things from getting too overwhelming, you're going to be building something you've already built. Hopefully, the powerful and expressive syntax of Rust will make the game easier to reason about, and you might even be able to add features and rules that weren't in the last game.

This new version of checkers will expose the same kinds of functions to the host (JavaScript), but you'll also be writing some code that determines the list of valid moves, something that was just too excruciatingly painful in raw wast code to write in the previous chapter. The Rust version will also have the same concept of turns so that it can be played from a console or virtually any other kind of client.

To get started, find an empty directory and type the following:

```
$ cargo new --lib rustycheckers
Created library `rustycheckers` project
```

Edit the Cargo.toml file in the project's root directory as you did for the last sample to tell the build system that this is a dynamic library. Once you've got that set up, you should be ready to start coding. If you're using a version of Rust version 1.31.0 or newer, then your default Cargo.toml will come with a line in the package section: edition = "2018". This indicates the use of the "2018 edition"[5] which allows for some newer (and often simpler) syntax, as well as many new features.

---

5.   rust-lang-nursery.github.io/edition-guide/rust-2018/index.html

Make sure you remove this line from your Cargo.toml. For now, I want to focus on the core parts of Rust required to interact with WebAssembly, and will defer the use of the 2018 edition until the end of the book after you've had time to get used to the "regular" Rust syntax. Unless otherwise stated, all Rust samples in this book are designed to run on 1.31.0 or newer, but use the "2015 edition" syntax.

Setting Up the Board

Open up the rustycheckers/src/lib.rs file and empty it. At the bottom of the file, add the following line:

```
mod board;
```

Now add a file called rustycheckers/src/board.rs. Rust's module system is hierarchical. Wherever you add mod [module_name]; in your code, think of that module as being *injected* at exactly that spot in the hierarchy. This allows you to nest modules, and it fosters some really good isolation and encapsulation practices, but it can be hard to get used to for people who come from languages with implicit or directory-first module hierarchies.

Each Rust library has a single root module, the name of which is specified in the Cargo.toml file (the name setting under the [package] section). By convention, the code for the root module is found in the lib.rs file, so by including mod board; in the top of lib.rs, we're declaring a submodule named board that exists directly under the root. Elements in the board submodule can be referenced from anywhere using the rustycheckers::board prefix.

The Rust 2018 edition[6] (not used until the end of this book) has more flexible rules around referring to modules.

To start writing the code to manage the game board, the first thing you'll want to do is write some code to manage a GamePiece. In the previous chapter, game pieces were just 32-bit integers that could be bitmasked for information. Now that you've got a little more power to play with, you can create an enum for piece color and a struct (Rust doesn't officially have classes, though its structs can often behave like classes) to represent a single piece:

rustycheckers/src/board.rs
```
#[derive(Debug, Copy, Clone, PartialEq)]
pub enum PieceColor {
    White,
    Black,
}
```

---

6. rust-lang-nursery.github.io/edition-guide/rust-2018/module-system/index.html

```
#[derive(Debug, Clone, Copy, PartialEq)]
pub struct GamePiece {
    pub color: PieceColor,
    pub crowned: bool,
}

impl GamePiece {
    pub fn new(color: PieceColor) -> GamePiece {
        GamePiece {
            color,
            crowned: false,
        }
    }

    pub fn crowned(p: GamePiece) -> GamePiece {
        GamePiece {
            color: p.color,
            crowned: true,
        }
    }
}
```

Don't worry about the derive macros for now. They just auto-generate some boilerplate code to deal with common things most data structures in Rust need, like the ability to be compared, copied, cloned, and printed out for debug purposes.

This game piece has two functions: new() and crowned(). The first creates a new game piece of a given color, while the second creates a new piece of a given color with a crown on top. The latter function will come in handy when you want to crown a piece on the board.

Next, you can create the concept of a Coordinate. In raw WebAssembly, you didn't have anything to represent this other than just numbers. Creating a struct for a grid coordinate here should help simplify the code, reduce the number of parameters that get passed around, and generally make things more readable. Also, as you'll see, it's a great place to stick some preliminary logic to support game rules:

rustycheckers/src/board.rs
```
#[derive(Debug, Clone, PartialEq, Copy)]
pub struct Coordinate(pub usize, pub usize);

impl Coordinate {
    pub fn on_board(self) -> bool {
        let Coordinate(x, y) = self;
        x <= 7 && y <= 7
    }
```

❷
```rust
    pub fn jump_targets_from(&self) -> impl Iterator<Item = Coordinate> {
        let mut jumps = Vec::new();
        let Coordinate(x, y) = *self;
        if y >= 2 {
            jumps.push(Coordinate(x + 2, y - 2));
        }
        jumps.push(Coordinate(x + 2, y + 2));

        if x >= 2 && y >= 2 {
            jumps.push(Coordinate(x - 2, y - 2));
        }
        if x >= 2 {
            jumps.push(Coordinate(x - 2, y + 2));
        }
        jumps.into_iter()
    }
```

❸
```rust
    pub fn move_targets_from(&self) -> impl Iterator<Item = Coordinate> {
        let mut moves = Vec::new();
        let Coordinate(x, y) = *self;
        if x >= 1 {
            moves.push(Coordinate(x - 1, y + 1));
        }
        moves.push(Coordinate(x + 1, y + 1));
        if y >= 1 {
            moves.push(Coordinate(x + 1, y - 1));
        }
        if x >= 1 && y >= 1 {
            moves.push(Coordinate(x - 1, y - 1));
        }
        moves.into_iter()
    }
}
```

❶ An example of destructuring to pull the x and y values out of a Coordinate structure.

❷ Produce an iterator of Coordinates of all possible jumps from the given coordinate.

❸ Produce an iterator of Coordinates of all possible moves from the given coordinate.

The jump_targets_from() function returns a list of *potential* jump targets from the given coordinate. The move_targets_from() function returns a list of potential move (adjacent space) targets given the current coordinate location. These functions will be used to calculate a list of valid moves for each turn. Note that in the raw WebAssembly version of checkers, we just did a quick, naive check to verify that a move was valid. We can up the complexity a little here.

The code pub struct Coordinate(pub usize, pub usize) defines what's called a *tuple struct*. Rather than this struct having named fields, it instead represents a strongly-typed tuple with public fields. You can access those fields with tuple accessors .0 and .1, but most of the code in this chapter uses destructuring and pattern matching to get at the x and y values in a more human-friendly fashion. In this case, each of the two anonymous fields in this tuple struct are of type usize, which is the data type Rust uses for vector indexes, allowing code to be more safe and portable across 32-bit and 64-bit architectures. Rust's standard library is replete with usages of this data type.

The list of potential target squares for a checker piece to move is pretty small. The preceding code creates *iterators* that expose these potential squares to callers. As you'll see shortly, iterators can be chained with functions like map(), zip(), and filter() to make for some fairly expressive syntax to define game rules.

Finish out the board.rs module by creating a struct that represents a game move. Here you can see one place where it was simpler to access the tuple values as fields rather than using a pattern match:

```
rustycheckers/src/board.rs
#[derive(Debug, Clone, PartialEq, Copy)]
pub struct Move {
    pub from: Coordinate,
    pub to: Coordinate,
}

impl Move {
    pub fn new(from: (usize, usize), to: (usize, usize)) -> Move {
        Move {
            from: Coordinate(from.0, from.1),
            to: Coordinate(to.0, to.1),
        }
    }
}
```

One more thing before getting into the details of writing the game rules: *references*. In the coordinate code, &self is a reference to the struct. In Rust, anything prefixed with & is a reference. Any assignment that isn't a reference is a *move*. Unless you explicitly treat something as a reference, ownership will be transferred during an assignment, meaning the value in the "old" variable will no longer be there (and you'll get a compile error if you try to access it). This "move by default" pattern takes a bit of getting used to when learning Rust, and if the difference between move and reference is a little murky, you might want to take a minute and do a little background research on Rust's concept of ownership.[7]

Writing the Engine Rules

Now for the fun part... open up rustycheckers/src/lib.rs and add the following line of code to the bottom:

```
mod game;
```

Create an empty file called rustycheckers/src/game.rs. This will give you a nice clean space to work on the game rules, and it illustrates a pretty common pattern in idiomatic Rust: modularization. I am partial to small, purposeful files that are easy to read and understand, and I feel like I spend more time thinking about modular structure in Rust than I have in other languages I've used (which is a good thing).

The first thing you'll want is a struct to anchor all of the game engine functionality to the same place, and to give you a spot to maintain game state. If you hadn't noticed, thus far you haven't done anything remotely related to WebAssembly, and that's deliberate. You'll want to keep the WebAssembly border clear of debris and make sure that you are free to build a game on this side of the Wasm/Rust border with very little crossover or coupling.

Patterns like this where we actively avoid tightly coupling two separate concerns allow our code to be easier to read, easier to maintain, and easier to add more features and use for unintended consumers in the future without modification. This kind of tactic is often referred to as a *facade* or an *Anti-Corruption Layer*.

```
rustycheckers/src/game.rs
use super::board::{Coordinate, GamePiece, Move, PieceColor};

pub struct GameEngine {
    board: [[Option<GamePiece>; 8]; 8],
    current_turn: PieceColor,
    move_count: u32,
}
pub struct MoveResult {
    pub mv: Move,
    pub crowned: bool,
}
```

In the previous chapter, you managed game state by manipulating bytes with direct memory access. Here, not only do you have a traditional two-dimensional

---

7. doc.rust-lang.org/book/ch04-00-understanding-ownership.html

array, but the type of the piece is Option<GamePiece>. It will make your code eminently more readable when an empty square is represented by the match-friendly keyword None rather than just a 0.

Remembering that the functionality for a struct resides in an impl block, start writing the code to initialize the game engine and its state inside the impl GameEngine block:

rustycheckers/src/game.rs
```
impl GameEngine {
    pub fn new() -> GameEngine {
        let mut engine = GameEngine {
            board: [[None; 8]; 8],
            current_turn: PieceColor::Black,
            move_count: 0,
        };
        engine.initialize_pieces();
        engine
    }

    pub fn initialize_pieces(&mut self) {
        [1, 3, 5, 7, 0, 2, 4, 6, 1, 3, 5, 7]
            .iter()
            .zip([0, 0, 0, 0, 1, 1, 1, 1, 2, 2, 2, 2].iter())
            .map(|(a, b)| (*a as usize, *b as usize))
            .for_each(|(x, y)| {
                self.board[x][y] = Some(GamePiece::new(PieceColor::White));
            });

        [0, 2, 4, 6, 1, 3, 5, 7, 0, 2, 4, 6]
            .iter()
            .zip([5, 5, 5, 5, 6, 6, 6, 6, 7, 7, 7, 7].iter())
            .map(|(a, b)| (*a as usize, *b as usize))
            .for_each(|(x, y)| {
                self.board[x][y] = Some(GamePiece::new(PieceColor::Black));
            });
    }
}
```

The &mut self parameter to initialize_pieces() indicates that it can only be used by a mutable reference to a game engine. Further, it's a sign to any developer that this function mutates state. In the engine's constructor, we create a mutable instance of the GameEngine struct, and then call initialize_pieces() to set the board up for play.

This function might seem confusing if you're not used to Rust syntax. In the previous chapter, you initialized the board by manually placing every single piece with a different line of code. In the real world, we have tools like iterators and filters that can help us with these tasks.

The iter() function converts an array of known x- or y-coordinate positions into an iterator, which can then be zipped (a function that merges two iterators into an iterator of tuples) with another iterator via the zip() function. Next, the map() function converts the coordinates from i32 to usize (the data type for array indexes in Rust—remember Rust doesn't have implicit conversions). For each one of the newly zipped (x,y) coordinates, you can set the appropriate black or white piece using Rust's anonymous function notation.

The next bit of code takes a top-down approach and contains the logic to move pieces on the board. If you enter this by hand right now, it won't compile because you're missing a bunch of helper functions. But I think it's easier to understand what's happening by looking at this logic first:

rustycheckers/src/game.rs
```
pub fn move_piece(&mut self, mv: &Move) -> Result<MoveResult, ()> {
    let legal_moves = self.legal_moves();

    if !legal_moves.contains(mv) {
        return Err(());
    }

    let Coordinate(fx, fy) = mv.from;
    let Coordinate(tx, ty) = mv.to;
    let piece = self.board[fx][fy].unwrap();
    let midpiece_coordinate = self.midpiece_coordinate(fx, fy, tx, ty);
    if let Some(Coordinate(x, y)) = midpiece_coordinate {
        self.board[x][y] = None; // remove the jumped piece
    }

    // Move piece from source to dest
    self.board[tx][ty] = Some(piece);
    self.board[fx][fy] = None;

    let crowned = if self.should_crown(piece, mv.to) {
        self.crown_piece(mv.to);
        true
    } else {
        false
    };
    self.advance_turn();

    Ok(MoveResult {
        mv: mv.clone(),
        crowned: crowned,
    })
}
```

The first thing move_piece() does is compute the list of legal moves based on whose turn it is and the state of the game board. If the intended move isn't in the list of legal moves (this is why you need the derive macros to generate equality tests for the structs), then the function quits early.

There's a line of code in this function that uses the unwrap() function. Ordinarily we shy away from this, but since we know that accessing that one piece will work because of validation, we can get away with it. In a production application and adhering to defensive coding practices, we would probably validate this instead of calling unwrap().

Next, the engine checks to see if there's a game piece to jump on the way from the source to the destination coordinate. If there is, the jumped piece is removed from the board. The engine then performs the piece move by setting the old location to None. Finally, the function finishes by checking if it should crown the piece after it moved. Can you imagine how hard it would be to read or write the jump logic code in raw wast?

The move_piece() function returns a Result. Similar to an Option, a Result can have two values: either Ok(...) or Err(...). Using a pattern match on a result is a clean way to handle and propagate errors back up the call stack. Pattern matching against optional values or result types is something that you might be familiar with if you've developed with functional programming languages or used functional programming styles.

Computing Legal Moves

Computing the list of legal moves is the most complicated thing this Rust code does. In the following code, legal_moves() loops through every space on the board and then computes a list of valid moves from that position. This way, this function returns a list of every valid move that the current player can make (rusty checkers doesn't support multi-jumps to try to keep the codebase legible and book-friendly).

rustycheckers/src/game.rs

```
fn legal_moves(&self) -> Vec<Move> {
    let mut moves: Vec<Move> = Vec::new();
    for col in 0..8 {
        for row in 0..8 {
            if let Some(piece) = self.board[col][row] {
                if piece.color == self.current_turn {
                    let loc = Coordinate(col, row);
                    let mut vmoves = self.valid_moves_from(loc);
                    moves.append(&mut vmoves);
                }
            }
        }
    }
}
```

```
        moves
}
fn valid_moves_from(&self, loc: Coordinate) -> Vec<Move> {
    let Coordinate(x, y) = loc;
    if let Some(p) = self.board[x][y] {
        let mut jumps = loc
            .jump_targets_from()
            .filter(|t| self.valid_jump(&p, &loc, &t))
            .map(|ref t| Move {
                from: loc.clone(),
                to: t.clone(),
            }).collect::<Vec<Move>>();
        let mut moves = loc
            .move_targets_from()
            .filter(|t| self.valid_move(&p, &loc, &t))
            .map(|ref t| Move {
                from: loc.clone(),
                to: t.clone(),
            }).collect::<Vec<Move>>();
        jumps.append(&mut moves);
        jumps
    } else {
        Vec::new()
    }
}
```

There's an interesting pattern used in the valid_moves_from() function that uses the iterator functions created earlier and chains those results through filter(), map(), and collect():

```
let mut moves = loc
  .move_targets_from()
  .filter(|t| self.valid_move(&p, &loc, &t))
  .map(|ref t| Move {
      from: loc.clone(),
      to: t.clone(),
  }).collect::<Vec<Move>>();
```

This takes all of the potential move targets and filters them based on whether that target is a valid move for a given game piece, at a given location, for a given target. Then, for each of the valid moves, we convert the coordinate target (indicated by the ref t in the lambda, showing that we're taking the lambda's sole parameter by *reference*) into a Move struct. Finally, the resulting iterator is converted into a vector via collect() and the "turbofish"[8] syntax collect::<Vec<Move>>().

---

8. doc.rust-lang.org/book/2018-edition/appendix-02-operators.html?highlight=turbo#non-operator-symbols

The valid_moves_from() function produces a list of Move instances that are valid from the given coordinate. In formal checkers, if a player has both a valid jump and a valid move, they must perform the jump. This method is structured to place valid jumps first so that you can add that kind of strict rule checking if you want. You could also add a new property to the Move struct to tag a move as a jump, which might help in adding multi-jump capabilities to the game.

You still haven't added anything to the code that deals with WebAssembly. In the interest of saving a few trees (or bytes), the full listings for all of the various helper functions like valid_move() aren't in the book. If you want the full source for board.rs and game.rs, you can grab it from the book's full example code. You'll also see several unit tests in the full version of the code that shows how you can test this code without crossing the WebAssembly boundary.

Coding the Rusty Checkers WebAssembly Interface

So far you've been coding in pure Rust without any indication that the game will eventually be available as a WebAssembly module. This is actually a good practice to adopt, and I'm a very big fan of keeping the boundary-crossing code at the edges, leaving the domain-specific code (in our case, checkers) in its own separate module to test in isolation.

You'll need to do two things to make this code work with a JavaScript host. First, you'll need to export functions that can be called by the host. Second, you'll need to import functions that you want to be called by the WebAssembly code on the host. This follows the same pattern as the previous chapter, but with stricter boundaries.

First, add the following two dependencies to your Cargo.toml file:

```
[dependencies]
mut_static = "5.0.0"
lazy_static = "1.0.2"
```

Rust is ruthless about its control over shared mutability, and here arises a conflict in philosophies. The previous raw WebAssembly module had global, module-wide state. How can you accomplish the same thing in Rust without violating all of its rules about sharing and mutability?

You're going to use something called a *lazy static* to create a globally available instance of the GameEngine struct. This instance will then be used by all of the functions you're exporting out of the WebAssembly module. The following code creates a lazy static game engine. Put it at the top of lib.rs:

rustycheckers/src/lib.rs
```
#[macro_use]
extern crate lazy_static;

use board::{Coordinate, GamePiece, Move, PieceColor};
use game::GameEngine;
use mut_static::MutStatic;

lazy_static! {
    pub static ref GAME_ENGINE: MutStatic<GameEngine> =
        { MutStatic::from(GameEngine::new()) };
}
```

In nearly every single case when writing Rust code, I would vehemently and aggressively push against the use of global mutable state. It goes against everything that Rust stands for, is bad for the environment, and makes puppies cry. However, in our edge case, like providing a mutable state store for a WebAssembly module, it is pretty much the only way to make the module work.

If you recall from the previous chapter, you exported a couple of functions out of your wat file to allow the host to query the state of the game: get_piece() and get_current_turn(). You'll rewrite those now:

rustycheckers/src/lib.rs
```
#[no_mangle]
pub extern "C" fn get_piece(x: i32, y: i32) -> i32 {
    let engine = GAME_ENGINE.read().unwrap();

    let piece = engine.get_piece(Coordinate(x as usize, y as usize));
    match piece {
        Ok(Some(p)) => p.into(),
        Ok(None) => -1,
        Err(_) => -1,
    }
}

#[no_mangle]
pub extern "C" fn get_current_turn() -> i32 {
    let engine = GAME_ENGINE.read().unwrap();

    GamePiece::new(engine.current_turn()).into()
}
```

To maintain the safety of the globally mutable game engine, you have to acquire a read or write lock with the read() or write() functions.

Since there's a chance that acquiring one of these locks can fail, those functions return Results. You have to handle results one way or another, and here calling unwrap() either grabs the value within Ok(...) or crashes the program upon failure. A tip learned from painful experience: in production-grade applications, seek out and destroy all unwrap()s with very few exceptions. Being unable to acquire a read or write lock on your game's sole source of state is, however, something that is exceptional and should produce a trap for the host.

The raw version of the checkers module you wrote returned the current piece and the current turn owners both as i32 values. As mentioned at the beginning of the chapter, you'll adhere to this contract wherever possible. If you look at both of these functions, you may notice that they both make use of a function called into().

The into() function shows one of my favorite aspects of Rust in action. Anything that implements the generic trait called Into<T> for a given type can be converted *into* that type. While Rust doesn't have implicit conversions, its *explicit* conversions are quite powerful. To convert a game piece into a 32-bit integer, you just need to implement Into<i32>:

```
rustycheckers/src/lib.rs
const PIECEFLAG_BLACK: u8 = 1;
const PIECEFLAG_WHITE: u8 = 2;
const PIECEFLAG_CROWN: u8 = 4;

impl Into<i32> for GamePiece {
    fn into(self) -> i32 {
        let mut val: u8 = 0;
        if self.color == PieceColor::Black {
            val += PIECEFLAG_BLACK;
        } else if self.color == PieceColor::White {
            val += PIECEFLAG_WHITE;
        }

        if self.crowned {
            val += PIECEFLAG_CROWN;
        }

        val as i32
    }
}
```

The fact that the self variable here is not a reference means that the GamePiece will be *consumed* when converted into an integer. In other words, if you try to access a game piece after you convert it into an integer, you'll get a compilation error with a message like "move after use," and an arrow pointing to the spot where you used it and where it moved. Rust's compiler errors are some of the most verbose and helpful I've ever seen.

There are some cool Rust libraries that help you do bit flags, but aren't really needed for this sample. Next, add a function to let players move:

rustycheckers/src/lib.rs

```
#[no_mangle]
pub extern "C" fn move_piece(fx: i32, fy: i32, tx: i32, ty: i32) -> i32 {
    let mut engine = GAME_ENGINE.write().unwrap();
    let mv = Move::new((fx as usize, fy as usize), (tx as usize, ty as usize));
    let res = engine.move_piece(&mv);
    match res {
        Ok(mr) => {
            unsafe {
                notify_piecemoved(fx, fy, tx, ty);
            }
            if mr.crowned {
                unsafe {
                    notify_piececrowned(tx, ty);
                }
            }
            1
        }
        Err(_) => 0,
    }
}
```

The move_piece() function (it can't be called move() because that's a reserved word in Rust) just forwards the call to the game engine and examines the result. It does, however, call the two notification functions that need to be imported from the host: notify_piecemoved() and notify_piececrowned(). These functions are both wrapped inside an unsafe block because Rust can't guarantee that the code on the other side of the host-module barrier meets Rust's standards for safety. Any extern function must be wrapped in an unsafe block to invoke it. It's a best practice to keep unsafe blocks as small as possible, wrapping only the thing you need to invoke.

Unsafe here shouldn't instill a sense of fear in you. This kind of unsafe is just an indicator the code you're invoking is unknown to the Rust compiler, so it can't give you the safety guarantees that you get from regular compiled Rust code.

Importing functions from a host is done by including their signatures in an extern block:

rustycheckers/src/lib.rs

```
extern "C" {
    fn notify_piecemoved(fromX: i32, fromY: i32,
                         toX: i32, toY: i32);
    fn notify_piececrowned(x: i32, y: i32);
}
```

Finally, you can compile this code for the WebAssembly target and create the stripped binary file suitable for use with JavaScript. The following commands will build your WebAssembly module and place the trimmed-down, release version in a demo directory (you'll need to create this directory yourself):

```
$ cargo build --release --target wasm32-unknown-unknown
Finished release [optimized] target(s) in 0.01s
$ cp target/wasm32-unknown-unknown/release/rustycheckers.wasm demo/
```

At this point, you've made a stack (definitely not a *heap*) of progress. You've got a Rust library that compiles to WebAssembly, imports notification functions, and exports functions that will let a host play a game of checkers while maintaining internal state. Next, you'll see how that works by testing out the game in a JavaScript host.

Playing Rusty Checkers in JavaScript

With just a few minor changes, your new Rust-built checkers WebAssembly module should work the same way as it did before. To get started, copy the index.html from the previous chapter into the demo directory.

Next, create the demo/index.js file and edit its contents to match the following:

```
rustycheckers/demo/index.js
fetch('./rustycheckers.wasm').then(response =>
  response.arrayBuffer()
).then(bytes => WebAssembly.instantiate(bytes, {
  env: {
    notify_piecemoved: (fX, fY, tX, tY) => {
      console.log("A piece moved from (" + fX + "," + fY +
        ") to (" + tX + "," + tY + ")");
    },
    notify_piececrowned: (x, y) => {
      console.log("A piece was crowned at (" + x + "," + y + ")");
    }
  },
}
)).then(results => {
  instance = results.instance;

  console.log("At start, current turn is " +
    instance.exports.get_current_turn());
  let piece = instance.exports.get_piece(0, 7);
  console.log("Piece at 0,7 is " + piece);

  let res = instance.exports.move_piece(0, 5, 1, 4); // B
  console.log("First move result: " + res);
  console.log("Turn after move: " + instance.exports.get_current_turn());
```

```
let bad = instance.exports.move_piece(1, 4, 2, 3); // illegal move
console.log("Illegal move result: " + bad);
console.log("Turn after illegal move: " +
  instance.exports.get_current_turn());
}).catch(console.error);
```

The first real difference between this JavaScript and the code from the previous chapter is that the object name wrapping the functions to be imported by the checkers module is env. In the previous chapter, you had control over the namespace name of the imports and called it events.

Rust code built for the wasm32-unknown-unknown target will default to putting function imports in the env namespace. It's not that big of an inconvenience, but being aware of subtleties like this can save you headaches in the future.

The rest of the code should look nearly identical, except that now when you attempt to make a truly illegal move, the new and improved code will catch it and return 0. Just for fun, see if you can set up a series of moves that allows a single jump so you can verify that a jump really does remove a piece from the board.

Wrapping Up

This chapter was fairly dense and covered a lot of material. You installed Rust, set up the wasm32-unknown-unknown target, and built a functioning checkers module with Rust. Now that you've experienced first-hand building the checkers module from scratch using nothing but wast syntax, you can compare and contrast that with building the same functionality with the additional benefits of Rust's strong type system, safety, and expressiveness.

So far, you've been spending nearly all of your time inside the WebAssembly module and little to no time working with the browser host. In the coming chapters, that's going to change as you unlock more features with tooling and code generation designed to bridge the gap between WebAssembly modules and their hosts. You'll start building real web applications with seamless user experiences.

CHAPTER 4

Integrating WebAssembly with JavaScript

So far, everything you've done in this book has been isolated almost entirely within the realm of WebAssembly. You've written a checkers engine in raw wast, then you wrote an upgraded one in Rust and compiled it to the wasm32-unknown-unknown target. Even though both of these projects had places where JavaScript could attach its tentacles, you can't really refer to either of those samples as tightly integrated.

In this chapter, you'll take a look at the Rust WebAssembly ecosystem, including the tooling and libraries available to help bridge the gap between WebAssembly and JavaScript. You'll start off by creating a new "Hello, World" template that illustrates a new way of communicating between JavaScript and Rust.

Next, you'll explore tools like *wasm-bindgen* that allow Rust to see JavaScript classes (and JavaScript to use Rust structures), expose and invoke callbacks in either language, send strings as function parameters, and return complex values, all while maintaining Rust's strict sharing rules.

By the end of the chapter, you'll not only know the mechanics of how to interoperate with JavaScript, but you'll have seen patterns and examples of when and where you should divide your logic up between JavaScript and Rust WebAssembly modules by building an interactive, browser-based game.

Creating a Better "Hello, World"

Most of the information in the book thus far can be applied universally to all kinds of WebAssembly applications written in all kinds of languages. That path diverges in this chapter. From here on out, everything in the book will be specific to Rust.

More importantly, everything you do after this point will rely on tools or libraries created by the Rust community. As interest in WebAssembly with

Rust grows, we can only expect this community to grow, and the power and usefulness of its tools and libraries to grow along with it. Even as young as WebAssembly is, you already have quite a few Rust tools at your disposal.

While you have a degree of choice when it comes to JavaScript bindings, the one that you'll be using in this chapter is *wasm-bindgen*[1]. This is a combination of a set of *crates* (Rust's name for shared libraries, though there's more nuance to them than that) that support *bindings* between JavaScript and Rust.

At its core, wasm-bindgen injects a bunch of metadata into your compiled WebAssembly module. Then, a separate command-line tool reads that metadata, strips it out, and uses that information to generate an appropriate JavaScript "wrapper bridge" containing the kinds of functions, classes, and other primitives that the developer wants bound to Rust.

Installing the New Tools

wasm-bindgen uses procedural macros and a few other features that at one point were only available in the *nightly* build of Rust. Thankfully, during the course of writing this book, Rust's support for those features is now stable.

Now that you're going to be writing a bit more JavaScript, you'll be using features that often call for the use of npm. Refer to the instructions[2] for your operating system to install Node and the Node Package Manager (npm).

Finally, you'll need to install the wasm-bindgen command-line tool. To do that, you'll use cargo, Rust's build tool:

```
$ cargo install wasm-bindgen-cli
```

If through previous experiments you've already installed wasm-bindgen and you want to force the installation of the latest version, add --force to the end of the cargo install command. This might take quite a while as there are a large number of dependencies and each one gets compiled after the source is downloaded.

Creating a New Rust WebAssembly Project

In this section you'll be creating a new WebAssembly module that makes use of wasm-bindgen bindings and its CLI, as well as webpack, npm, and a few other tools. As a self-identified "back end" developer, I get a little nervous when people mention all of these JavaScript build tools. Don't worry, though, we only need a few, and most of that is just to get a basic web server running. Also as a non-authority on JavaScript, JavaScript developers may find far

---

1. rustwasm.github.io/wasm-bindgen
2. www.npmjs.com/get-npm

more optimal ways of accomplishing some of the tasks in this chapter than the way I've outlined.

You'll go through the process of setting up this "Hello, World" piece by piece, and when you're done, you'll have a nice template that you can use as scaffolding to build future projects (which will come in handy in the second half of this chapter).

To start, create a new Rust project called bindgenhello (this is in the jsint_bindgenhello directory in the book's code samples) in a clean root directory:

```
$ cargo new bindgenhello --lib
```

This should look familiar. As with all the other Rust WebAssembly projects, you need to change its library type to cdylib in Cargo.toml. Also, add a reference to wasm-bindgen (and make sure you delete the "2018 edition" line if you have it):

jsint_bindgenhello/Cargo.toml
```
[package]
name = "bindgenhello"
version = "0.1.0"
authors = ["Your Name <your@address.com>"]

[lib]
crate-type = ["cdylib"]

[dependencies]
wasm-bindgen = "0.2"
```

The last time you went through this exercise, you created a simple function that performed addition. This time, you'll clean out the lib.rs file and replace it with the following:

jsint_bindgenhello/src/lib.rs
```
extern crate wasm_bindgen;
use wasm_bindgen::prelude::*;

// Import 'window.alert'
#[wasm_bindgen]
extern "C" {
    fn alert(s: &str);
}

// Export a 'hello' function
#[wasm_bindgen]
pub fn hello(name: &str) {
    alert(&format!("Hello, {}!", name));
}
```

Decorating Rust code with #[wasm_bindgen] triggers the invocation of a compile-time Rust *macro*. Each time the compiler encounters this macro, it generates some code on your behalf. Some of it will be code that winds up in your .wasm module, but some of it will be metadata used to help generate the corresponding JavaScript output produced by the wasm-bindgen command-line tool.

In this lib.rs file, there are two bindings. The first binds the alert() function to the alert() JavaScript function. With this binding in place, any Rust code that invokes the alert() function will be converted into a bunch of code that invokes the JavaScript alert() function from inside a WebAssembly module. Attaching the right window context and making all of the JavaScript pieces work properly is all done for us by wasm-bindgen.

The second binding exposes the hello() function. You've seen how this kind of function can be exposed before. However, in this case, it takes a *reference* to a string as a parameter. We know that string parameters aren't possible in pure WebAssembly, so the generated wrapper code produces the necessary plumbing (in both wast instructions and JavaScript boilerplate) to allow complex data to flow seamlessly between boundaries.

Behind the scenes, memory allocation and disposal functions are created that operate on the module's linear memory (remember the good old days when you had to do that by hand?). Then, each time wasm-bindgen encounters the need for string allocation, the generated JavaScript invokes those functions. In short, all of the hard work you've been doing in the past couple of chapters is now done automatically on your behalf. These wrappers are convenient, of course, but I still firmly believe that you are better off for having learned how things were done "the hard way."

Go ahead and build this to make sure that you get a valid WebAssembly module:

```
$ cargo build --target wasm32-unknown-unknown
```

There's one final piece to this compilation that you need to complete when you're using wasm-bindgen—invoke the CLI to produce a new WebAssembly module and a JavaScript wrapper file:

```
$ wasm-bindgen target/wasm32-unknown-unknown/debug/bindgenhello.wasm \
--out-dir .
```

This drops a new file, bindgenhello_bg.wasm, in the project directory. It also generates the wrapper JavaScript file, bindgenhello.js, and a TypeScript definition (bindgenhello.d.ts) in that directory. Since these are all generated, you might want to exclude them from your version control system, though checking generated code into VCS is actually a pretty nuanced subject, so your mileage may vary. I've included a build.sh script in the code samples that produces the .wasm file and then calls wasm-bindgen.

> ## Cargo Update
>
> Occasionally, when you go to build a project that built successfully the week before
> (or when this book's samples were generated, for instance), you may see weird errors
> in libraries that you didn't write. This happens sometimes with conflicts between
> locally cached builds and libraries pulled from the internet. *Most* of the time you
> should be able to resolve this by running cargo update and then attempting the build
> again. You may also be prompted to update if the versions of wasm-bindgen used in the
> CLI and in your .wasm module don't match.

The following function is auto-generated, but it's worth looking at the wrapper
function for hello():

```
export function hello(arg0) {
    const ptr0 = passStringToWasm(arg0);
    const len0 = WASM_VECTOR_LEN;
    try {
        return wasm.hello(ptr0, len0);
    } finally {
        wasm.__wbindgen_free(ptr0, len0 * 1);
    }
}
```

The memory offset and length of the allocated string are returned from a
function called passStringToWasm(). This function invokes the generated allocation
function inside the WebAssembly module, placing the encoded string in the
module's linear memory and then doing the relevant pointer arithmetic.
Having written your own wast code, you should be able to appreciate how great
it is to have this code generated on your behalf.

After the hello() function is done, the code will *free* the previously allocated
memory via the __wbindgen_free() function that wasm-bindgen stuffed into the
WebAssembly module for us. With the WebAssembly side of this "Hello, World"
done, it's time to move on to the JavaScript side of the house.

Integrating with JavaScript and npm

In order to run this sample in a browser like you did before, you'll need a web
server and some way of serving up your script content that invokes the wasm
module. In addition, for this sample, you're going to set up a *webpack* configuration. Follow the appropriate instructions to ensure you're using the latest
version of webpack. If you're a JavaScript pro (unlike myself), then feel free
to use whatever tooling feels most comfortable to you.

There are some handy shortcuts you can use with webpack to do things like automatically generate the index.html. To keep things simple and easier to understand, I'm deliberately not optimizing certain things in this book. You could also choose not to use webpack at all.

The real work happens in the index.js file. This is where it really pays to use additional tools. You can see that it looks like simple, clean, idiomatic JavaScript, even though it's going through a bridge to integrate with a WebAssembly module. It's truly the best of both worlds—the Rust code targeting WebAssembly looks like idiomatic Rust, and the JavaScript looks like standard, unmodified JavaScript:

jsint_bindgenhello/index.js
```
const wasm = import('./bindgenhello');

wasm
    .then(h => h.hello("world!"))
    .catch(console.error);
```

Next, set up a web pack configuration so that you can use it to manage your JavaScript bundles. Note that the entry point is index.js. Previous versions of this book required some shoe-horning and other shenanigans to get this working, but the WebAssembly ecosystem is always improving, and things are getting simpler every day:

jsint_bindgenhello/webpack.config.js
```
const path = require('path');
const HtmlWebpackPlugin = require('html-webpack-plugin');
const webpack = require('webpack');

module.exports = {
    entry: './index.js',
    output: {
        path: path.resolve(__dirname, 'dist'),
        filename: 'index.js',
    },
    plugins: [
        new HtmlWebpackPlugin(),
        // Have this example work in Edge which doesn't ship `TextEncoder` or
        // `TextDecoder` at this time.
        new webpack.ProvidePlugin({
            TextDecoder: ['text-encoding', 'TextDecoder'],
            TextEncoder: ['text-encoding', 'TextEncoder']
        })
    ],
    mode: 'development'
};
```

Finally, create a package.json file. In addition to setting up your webpack development web server, you could also use this as a place to automate your build process by calling the build.sh shell script or something similar:

```
jsint_bindgenhello/package.json
{
    "scripts": {
        "build": "webpack",
        "serve": "webpack-dev-server"
    },
    "devDependencies": {
        "text-encoding": "^0.7.0",
        "html-webpack-plugin": "^3.2.0",
        "webpack": "^4.11.1",
        "webpack-cli": "^3.1.1",
        "webpack-dev-server": "^3.1.0"
    }
}
```

Now you should be able to execute a build script to produce the WebAssembly module and the generated JavaScript files, then npm run serve to start the webpack server. Pointing your WebAssembly-enabled browser at your local host on port 8080 should then pop up a JavaScript alert dialog box. Try this out on your own and bask in the glow of autogenerated JavaScript interop goodness.

With this "Hello, World" project template in hand, it's time to move on to building something a little more powerful with the help of wasm-bindgen.

Building the Rogue WebAssembly Game

Back in the days before the Internet filled up with pictures of kittens, animated memes, and ubiquitous social networking, university students had to walk three miles uphill in the snow to computer labs so they could play games on monochrome monitors tethered to Unix servers.

One of these games was an incredible creation called Rogue.[3] Remember when I suggested that constraints are often good for innovation? Rogue is a fantastic example of that. Fed up with text games that you could only play once, Rogue's creators managed to let players hack and slash their way through procedurally generated dungeons in a simple 80 column by 24 row terminal.

For this code sample, you'll be taking a JavaScript library for creating Rogue-like games and building a game with it. The point of this exercise isn't to build a game (though that is a fun side effect), but rather to illustrate some possible

---

3. www.gamasutra.com/view/feature/4013/the_history_of_rogue_have__you_.php?print=1

ways for WebAssembly to interact with your JavaScript code and third-party JavaScript libraries. We want to examine strategies for spreading code and logic across the boundary between Rust (WebAssembly) and JavaScript.

It's important to prepare for our decision about where to draw those boundaries and how to spread the code to be wrong. We will make an attempt, see how it plays, see what the code looks like, and then decide how to refactor it from there. Perfect software isn't created, it comes from iteration and the deliberate choice of an imperfect starting point.

In the *Rogue WebAssembly* game, your objective is to find and open all of the treasure chests. Inside one of these chests is a WebAssembly module. You will have to find this module before the dreaded *Rust Borrow Checker* captures you!

Getting Started with Rot.js

Before getting started, you might want to take a few minutes to familiarize yourself with the *Rot.js*[4] library. You don't need to become an expert. Just take a look at some of the basic documentation. In short, Rot.js injects a virtual 80x24 (you can resize it) terminal window into an HTML canvas. With that in place, you can use methods like draw() to place characters on the map, and hook up a turn-based actor system. This library has far more functionality than you'll use for this simple example (but plenty of goodies to play with if you want to add on later).

You can get started by making a new copy of the better "Hello, World" from the previous section. I called my new directory roguewasm, but you can call yours whatever you like. Make sure you've got a build script that builds the wasm module and invokes the wasm-bindgen CLI. You can do this with a shell script or with changes to package.json. You won't need to add a reference to Rot.js for npm. Instead, add that reference to the index.html file, where it will be clear that this is a traditional, client-side JavaScript dependency. There are other ways to rely on these kinds of dependencies, but this isn't a JavaScript book so I will steer clear of them.

The game screen consists of the canvas area managed by Rot.js, a header for the game title, and a sidebar that will serve as an area to display the player's statistics. Here's a very simple index.html file that uses CSS flex grid to create those regions (it may be difficult to tell, but I am not a designer):

---

4. ondras.github.io/rot.js/manual/#intro

jsint_roguewasm/index.html

```html
<html>

<head>
    <meta content="text/html;charset=utf-8" http-equiv="Content-Type" />
    <title>Rogue WebAssembly</title>
    <script src="https://cdn.jsdelivr.net/npm/rot-js@2/dist/rot.js"></script>
    <style>
        .row {
            display: flex;
        }

        .row_cell {
            flex: 1
        }
    </style>
</head>

<body>
    <div class="row">
        <div class="row_cell" style="text-align:center;">
            <h1>Rogue WebAssembly</h1>
        </div>
    </div>
    <div class="row">
        <div class="row_cell" id="rogueCanvas">

        </div>
        <div class="row_cell" id="statsContainer" style="padding:15px;">
            <div class="row_cell" style="text-align:center;">
                <h2>Stats</h2>
            </div>
            <p>
                <span>
                    <b>HitPoints:</b>
                </span> 
                <span id="hitpoints">0</span> / 
                <span id="max_hitpoints">0</span>
            </p>
            <p>
                <span>
                    <b>Moves:</b>
                </span> 
                <span id="moves">0</span>
            </p>
        </div>
    </div>

    <script src='./bootstrap.js'></script>
</body>

</html>
```

The next decision you need to make is the hardest: what code will be in your JavaScript (e.g., index.js) and what code will be in the WebAssembly module? The right answer isn't always to put everything inside WebAssembly or Rust just because that's what's new and shiny. There are a couple of things that Rot.js does quite well, like implementing pathfinding and random dungeon generation, that you're not going to want to reinvent in WebAssembly.

Instead, you'll want to invoke that functionality from wherever it's most appropriate. Using wasm-bindgen, you can allow JavaScript classes to manifest in Rust and you can let Rust structs with functions appear as classes in JavaScript. To get started, let's work on the game engine's core logic and see how much of it can be implemented in Rust.

Before moving on to creating the game engine, you might want to have a look at the Rot.js tutorial.[5] This tutorial walks you through creating the all-JavaScript game on which *Rogue WebAssembly* is based. Skimming through this might help provide some context as to what you are building in the next section.

Creating the Game Engine

The game engine is subservient to the JavaScript in index.js. If you took a look at the Rot.js documentation, you may have noticed that the random dungeon generation works by taking a *callback* parameter. While there are a number of dungeon types available, the one we'll be using in this game is a *digger*.

Each time Rot.js *digs* a piece out of raw map material, it invokes the callback. This callback contains the x- and y-coordinates of the spot, and a value integer. The meaning of this field varies between dungeon types. In the case of Rogue WebAssembly, we only care about the 0-values (open space).

First you're going to want to set up some code blocks to hold your imports and exports. Because I'm either clairvoyant or I've written this sample multiple times, I know that you're going to need access to the alert() and console.log() JavaScript functions, as well as eventually a stats_updated() function for notifying the UI when a player's stats change:

```
jsint_roguewasm/src/lib.rs
#[macro_use]
extern crate serde_derive;

extern crate wasm_bindgen;
use std::collections::HashMap;
use wasm_bindgen::prelude::*;
```

---

5.   www.roguebasin.com/index.php?title=Rot.js_tutorial

```rust
#[wasm_bindgen]
extern "C" {
    fn alert(s: &str);

    #[wasm_bindgen(js_namespace = console)]
    fn log(s: &str);

    #[wasm_bindgen(module = "./index")]
    fn stats_updated(stats: JsValue);

    pub type Display;

    #[wasm_bindgen(method, structural, js_namespace = ROT)]
    fn draw(this: &Display, x: i32, y: i32, ch: &str);

    #[wasm_bindgen(method, structural, js_name = draw, js_namespace = ROT)]
    fn draw_color(this: &Display, x: i32, y: i32, ch: &str, color: &str);
}
```

With the log() function, notice that you can import functions from specific JavaScript namespaces (e.g., console). You can tell wasm-bindgen which JavaScript module contains the function you're going to import, as we do with the stats_updated() function.

Next is where some of this tooling starts to really shine. Rot.js contains a class called Display in the ROT namespace. By declaring the Display type inside the extern block, wasm-bindgen makes that type available to your code and generates everything necessary to communicate with it. Notice that we didn't put a namespace qualifier on the Display type, only the functions. wasm-bindgen builds types from the functions, which do have a namespace qualifier.

You will want access to two overloads of the draw() method: one that just renders a character in the default colors and the other that renders a character with an explicit color code. There's a *lot* going on here, so make sure you spend a few minutes taking in all of the code generation happening on your behalf.

By using the structural and method keywords in the wasm_bindgen macro, we are telling the macro and JavaScript boilerplate to take the method accessed on the Display type and call the decorated function in the WebAssembly module.

If in JavaScript you had wanted to call ROT.Display.draw(4,5,"@"), you can invoke the Rust function display.draw(4,5,"@") where display is a Rust variable that behaves like a struct with methods. As you'll see, your JavaScript code can pass in a reference to an initialized ROT.Display and your Rust code can use whatever methods on it you declare in your extern block.

To create an instance of a Rot.js display and pass it to an instance of our game engine, we're first going to need the Engine class. This is a struct we define in Rust (you'll see it shortly), and, thanks to the wasm-bindgen macro, we can import it as though it was just another JavaScript class:

```
import { Engine, PlayerCore } from './jsint_roguewasm';
```

Here, roguewasm is a JavaScript file produced when we run the wasm-bindgen CLI tool. PlayerCore is another struct-exported-as-class that you'll see shortly. The JavaScript code to create an instance of a Rot.js display and pass it to an instance of the game engine looks like this:

jsint_roguewasm/index.js
```
//          this.display = new ROT.Display();
this.display = new ROT.Display({ width: 125, height: 40 })
document.getElementById("rogueCanvas").appendChild(this.display.getContainer());

this.engine = new Engine(this.display);
```

With some of that connective tissue set up, it's time to create the game engine. The foundation of the game is map generation and map rendering, and Rot.js uses the dig() callback to allow your game engine to produce the game map. Here's the Rust code for the engine that handles the *dig* callback, updates its state, and renders an entire map:

```
#[wasm_bindgen]
pub struct Engine {
    display: Display,
    points: HashMap<GridPoint, String>,
    prize_location: Option<GridPoint>,
}

#[wasm_bindgen]
impl Engine {
    #[wasm_bindgen(constructor)]
    pub fn new(display: Display) -> Engine {
        Engine {
            display,
            points: HashMap::new(),
            prize_location: None,
        }
    }

    pub fn on_dig(&mut self, x: i32, y: i32, val: i32) {
        if val == 0 {
            let pt = GridPoint { x, y };
            self.points.insert(pt, ".".to_owned());
        }
    }

    pub fn draw_map(&self) {
```

```
        for (k, v) in &self.points {
            self.display.draw(k.x, k.y, &v);
        }
    }
}
```

The Engine struct owns a reference to the following: a ROT Display instance, a hash that maps grid coordinates to renderable characters, and the location of the hidden WebAssembly module. The constructor illustrates an important point: *Rust structs cannot be initialized with missing fields.* To deal with something that could be missing like the prize location (you'll write that code in a bit), we make use of Rust's Option type.

on_dig() adds the supplied grid coordinates to the points field. The draw_map() function may look a little strange to you if you're not used to Rust. In Rust, by default, for loops *take ownership* of the items over which they iterate. This means if you just casually loop over a collection, you can't just dish out references to those items to other functions (because you no longer own them). If you don't want to own (many in the community may also call this *consuming*) the collection, you can iterate over *references* to the items as indicated by the & sign.

Lastly, the draw_map() function invokes the draw() function on the Display instance. Rust knows that this opaque thing provided by the host (in our case, provided by JavaScript) has a three-parameter draw() function on it because we specified that in our extern block.

With some map-related engine functions available on the Engine struct, you can write some code in a JavaScript Game class that invokes the Rot.js map digger:

jsint_roguewasm/index.js
```
generateMap: function () {
    var digger = new ROT.Map.Digger();
    var freeCells = [];

    var digCallback = function (x, y, value) {
        if (!value) {
            var key = x + "," + y;
            freeCells.push(key);
        }
❶       this.engine.on_dig(x, y, value);
    }
    digger.create(digCallback.bind(this));

    this.generateBoxes(freeCells);
❷   this.engine.draw_map();

❸   this.player = this._createBeing(Player, freeCells);
    this.enemy = this._createBeing(Checko, freeCells);
},
```

❶ Invoke the on_dig() function on the Rust Engine struct.

❷ Invoke the draw_map() function on the Rust Engine struct.

❸ Here this refers to the Game class instance and we call a utility function to create an instance of either a player or an enemy to put on the map.

The aging JavaScript syntax to add functions to the Game class is to avoid using translators and to keep the code samples as simple and portable as possible. Feel free to convert this to your favorite syntax and use Babel or its ilk to transpile the code.

Now that the map rendering and storage of grid points is taken care of, it's time to move on to adding players, enemies, and the cherished hidden treasure: the WebAssembly module.

Adding Players, Enemies, and Treasure

As you've seen, one strategy for separating the implementation between Rust and JavaScript is to assign responsibilities by expertise or to avoid limitations. For example, it makes a lot of sense for the top-level JavaScript to initiate the game and any dependencies and then call into the WebAssembly module for whatever remains.

In this section, you're going to add support for the player, an enemy, and obtaining the treasure that might be hidden within the boxes (* on the map canvas). Here you'll see another strategy for separating the two worlds: *encapsulation.*

Using encapsulation allows you to create a class called Player in JavaScript, and then have a private member inside that class that's an instance of the Rust-based *player core*. With this strategy, it becomes easy to have JavaScript handle things like keyboard input and configure the callbacks for use with Rot.js, all while deferring logic and other processing to the internal WebAssembly module.

This also lets you have a Player and Enemy class both share the functionality of the Rust-exported PlayerCore class. The JavaScript player class will handle subscribing to the *key down* browser event, exposing the Rot.js scheduler callback function act(), and exposing property queries and self-rendering functions. Let's take a look at the player abstraction in JavaScript:

```
jsint_roguewasm/index.js
var Player = function (x, y) {
    this._core = new PlayerCore(x, y, "@", "#ff0", Game.display);
    this._core.draw();
}
```

```javascript
Player.prototype.act = function () {
    Game.rotengine.lock();
    window.addEventListener("keydown", this);
}
Player.prototype.handleEvent = function (e) {
    var keyMap = {};
    keyMap[38] = 0;
    keyMap[33] = 1;
    keyMap[39] = 2;
    keyMap[34] = 3;
    keyMap[40] = 4;
    keyMap[35] = 5;
    keyMap[37] = 6;
    keyMap[36] = 7;

    var code = e.keyCode;

    if (code == 13 || code == 32) {
        Game.engine.open_box(this._core, this._core.x(), this._core.y());
        return;
    }

    /* one of numpad directions? */
    if (!(code in keyMap)) { return; }

    /* is there a free space? */
    var dir = ROT.DIRS[8][keyMap[code]];
    var newX = this._core.x() + dir[0];
    var newY = this._core.y() + dir[1];

    if (!Game.engine.free_cell(newX, newY)) { return; };

    Game.engine.move_player(this._core, newX, newY);
    window.removeEventListener("keydown", this);
    Game.rotengine.unlock();
}

Player.prototype.getX = function () { return this._core.x(); }

Player.prototype.getY = function () { return this._core.y(); }
```

The first interesting piece of JavaScript is this:

```javascript
this._core = new PlayerCore(x, y, "@", "#ff0", Game.display);
this._core.draw();
```

This creates an instance of the PlayerCore class, which is actually a Rust struct you'll write shortly that, through the power of wasm_bindgen, looks to JavaScript like an ordinary class. This constructor also takes an instance of a ROT.Display object, which gives the player core access to the map canvas.

If the key pressed by the player is a directional key, then Rot.js provides a convenience array (ROT.DIRS[8]) to help in computing the x- and y-coordinates of the direction indicated by a key press. In the following code, you can see the elements of the resulting direction array being added to the location state being managed by the player core:

```
var dir = ROT.DIRS[8][keyMap[code]];
var newX = this._core.x() + dir[0];
var newY = this._core.y() + dir[1];
```

This is a perfect example of some code better left in JavaScript. Rot.js already has facilities for direction calculation and, as you'll see, pathfinding, so there's no need to reinvent those in Rust.

If the key pressed isn't a movement key, but it's instead either the carriage return (code 13) or the space bar (code 32), then the player will try to open a box. This code defers to the WebAssembly module by invoking the Rust open_box() function on the Engine struct.

With the player's basic behavior defined, it's time to create the enemy. In this game, the player's arch-nemesis is the cruel, evil, heartless *borrow checker*, a villain responsible for ensuring your code can never be compiled unless it is memory safe! Let's call him *Checko*.

jsint_roguewasm/index.js
```
// Checko the Borrow Checker! Run away!
var Checko = function (x, y) {
    this._core = new PlayerCore(x, y, "B", "red", Game.display);
    this._core.draw();

    Checko.prototype.act = function () {
        var x = Game.player.getX();
        var y = Game.player.getY();

        var passableCallback = function (x, y) {
            return Game.engine.free_cell(x, y);
        }
        var astar = new ROT.Path.AStar(x, y, passableCallback, { topology: 4 });

        var path = [];
        var pathCallback = function (x, y) {
            path.push([x, y]);
        }
        astar.compute(this._core.x(), this._core.y(), pathCallback);

        path.shift();
        if (path.length <= 1) {
            Game.rotengine.lock();
            alert("Game over - you were captured by the Borrow Checker!!");
        } else {
```

```
            x = path[0][0];
            y = path[0][1];
            Game.engine.move_player(this._core, x, y);
        }
    }
}
```

Where the player's act() callback (invoked by the Rot.js scheduler) handles keyboard input and subsequent movement, *Checko the Borrow Checker*'s act() callback uses Rot.js's *A-star* pathfinding to compute a path to the player. It then finds the first step in that path and moves in that direction. If the path indicates that the player is about to be caught by Checko, the game is over. (Game.rotengine.lock() stops all schedulers.)

Again, you can see where the PlayerCore struct is maintaining Checko's current position. These coordinates are passed as initialization parameters to the A-star pathfinding algorithm. This calculation requires a callback, where the boolean indicator of whether a coordinate is traversable is deferred to the free_cell() function on the Engine struct (dots and asterisks are traverseable):

```
pub fn free_cell(&self, x: i32, y: i32) -> bool {
    let g = GridPoint { x, y };
    match self.points.get(&g) {
        Some(v) => v == "." || v == "*",
        None => false,
    }
}
```

Earlier in this section, you saw some code at the top of the lib.rs file that looked like this:

```
#[macro_use]
extern crate serde_derive;
```

This is a reference to the *serde* crate (*serde* refers to *serialization/de-serial-ization*). Serde is one of the most commonly used Rust crates in the entire ecosystem and contains functionality for manually performing raw serialization as well as macros for automatically deriving serialization and de-serialization implementations for your structs and enums.

As a reminder, the stats_updated() function provided by the browser host to be invoked by our game engine is declared as follows:

```
#[wasm_bindgen(module = "./index")]
fn stats_updated(stats: JsValue);
```

When the game engine invokes the stats_updated() callback, it's sending a raw JSON value rather than attempting to marshal a struct that exists on both sides of the barrier. This makes the stats notification faster and consume less resources because you don't need the generated boilerplate to make the Stats struct appear as a JavaScript class.

For this kind of serialization code to compile, you'll need to customize your Cargo.toml slightly so that the wasm-bindgen reference includes serialization support:

jsint_roguewasm/Cargo.toml
```
[package]
name = "roguewasm"
version = "0.1.0"
authors = ["Your Name <your@address.com>"]

[lib]
crate-type = ["cdylib"]

[dependencies]
serde = "^1.0.59"
serde_derive = "^1.0.59"

[dependencies.wasm-bindgen]
version = "^0.2"
features = ["serde-serialize"]
```

Now let's write the code for the player core and show some of the other important structs like Stats and GridPoint:

jsint_roguewasm/src/lib.rs
```
#[derive(Serialize)]
pub struct Stats {
    pub hitpoints: i32,
    pub max_hitpoints: i32,
    pub moves: i32,
}

#[derive(PartialEq, Eq, PartialOrd, Clone, Debug, Hash)]
struct GridPoint {
    pub x: i32,
    pub y: i32,
}

#[wasm_bindgen]
pub struct PlayerCore {
    loc: GridPoint,
    moves: i32,
    display: Display,
    hp: i32,
    max_hp: i32,
    icon: String,
    color: String,
}
```

```rust
#[wasm_bindgen]
impl PlayerCore {
    #[wasm_bindgen(constructor)]
    pub fn new(x: i32, y: i32, icon: &str,
            color: &str, display: Display) -> PlayerCore {
        PlayerCore {
            loc: GridPoint { x, y },
            display,
            moves: 0,
            max_hp: 100,
            hp: 100,
            icon: icon.to_owned(),
            color: color.to_owned(),
        }
    }

    pub fn x(&self) -> i32 {
        self.loc.x
    }

    pub fn y(&self) -> i32 {
        self.loc.y
    }

    pub fn draw(&self) {
        &self
            .display
            .draw_color(self.loc.x, self.loc.y, &self.icon, &self.color);
    }

    pub fn move_to(&mut self, x: i32, y: i32) {
        self.loc = GridPoint { x, y };
        self.draw();

        self.moves += 1;
        self.emit_stats();
    }

    pub fn emit_stats(&self) {
        let stats = Stats {
            hitpoints: self.hp,
            max_hitpoints: self.max_hp,
            moves: self.moves,
        };
        stats_updated(JsValue::from_serde(&stats).unwrap());
    }

    pub fn take_damage(&mut self, hits: i32) -> i32 {
        self.hp = self.hp - hits;
        self.emit_stats();
        self.hp
    }
}
```

The first arrow shows that every instance of a PlayerCore maintains the current location, icon, and icon color of the player (or enemy) that it supports. The second highlight shows internal state being converted into a struct that will be serialized as a raw JSON value and sent to the JavaScript host.

I'm not just showing my preference for encapsulation over inheritance with this implementation, but also illustrating a good pattern for hiding the seams between JS and WebAssembly. To make sure you've got a fully working version of the game to play with, download it from this book's resources. In the project directory, type:

```
$ npm install
...
$ npm run serve

> @ serve /home/kevin/Code/Rust/wasmbook/khrust/Book/code/jsint_roguewasm
> webpack-dev-server

i 「wds」: Project is running at http://localhost:8080/
i 「wds」: webpack output is served from /
i 「wdm」: Hash: 54b422da54fec6fc085e
Version: webpack 4.16.3

...
```

With your WebAssembly module compiled and processed by wasm-bindgen, you can now open localhost:8080 and you should be able to play Rogue WebAssembly and see a page that looks similar to this:

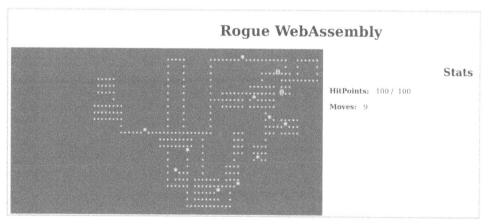

Congratulations—you've just created a micro version of one of the most classic and influential games of all time using WebAssembly and Rust! Before continuing to the next section of this chapter, you should, as usual, take a moment to bask in the glory of your own success and play the game. Keep an eye out for things that work, things that feel awkward, and what you like and don't like about it.

Experimenting Further

Rogue WebAssembly is far from perfect. There are plenty of areas for improvement: we can clean up the code, refactor methods, and make different choices with regard to the allocation of responsibilities between WebAssembly and JavaScript.

Before moving on to the next chapter, it might be worth your time to make some changes to the game. Experiment with moving more logic and state into the Rust code to try to keep the outer index.js as small as possible. What other features do you think would make the game more interesting? Try giving players the ability to fight each other by adding support for it in the PlayerCore Rust struct. Given the Rot.js scheduler system, can you add more NPCs (Non-Player Characters) to the game?

Your end result might not be a best-selling AAA-grade game, but playing around with this framework, experimenting with new things, and, most importantly, breaking it and trying to fix it, will give you invaluable muscle memory when it comes to writing Rust code and troubleshooting WebAssembly applications.

Using the js_sys Crate

At the top of the lib.rs file you wrote for the game, there are some externs declared that map to existing JavaScript functions, namely alert() and console.log(). It would get very tedious very quickly if you wanted your Rust code to have access to more native JavaScript functions and you had to manually write each one of those extern bindings.

Thankfully you don't have to write those bindings yourself. The work has already been done for you in the js_sys[6] crate. This crate, which is part of wasm-bindgen, contains all of the mappings you need to global JavaScript functions. Instead of manually defining the binding for alert() like you did in this chapter, you can simply call js_sys::alert(). Not only has all this work been done for you, but it saves you the trouble of figuring out exactly how to map the data types and parameters.

---

6.   rustwasm.github.io/wasm-bindgen/api/js_sys/

In the process of improving your copy of Rogue WebAssembly, go through and see if there are spots where you might be able to clean up the Rust or JavaScript code by making js_sys calls.

But wait, there's more! For the low price of *nothing*, you also get access to the web_sys crate! This crate has *all* of the JavaScript Web API bindings[7] in it. Your rust code can make web_sys calls and, at runtime, the JavaScript host will make web API calls on your behalf. Hopefully, at this point, you're starting to think that you have supervillain-like powers at your fingertips and you're feeling inspired to build your next world domination strategy in WebAssembly and Rust.

Wrapping Up

In this chapter, you took the giant leap from manual and cumbersome communication between JavaScript and Rust-based WebAssembly modules to using the wasm_bindgen crate. With this library's macros and command-line tooling, you have seamless, bi-directional invocations across the WebAssembly/JavaScript boundary.

To see this power in action, you built the Rogue WebAssembly game to help guide and inform your decisions about when code belongs in JavaScript versus when it belongs in Rust. Continuing this path toward more advanced tooling and libraries, in the next chapter, you'll get to build a fully functional, networked, multi-user application almost entirely in Rust.

---

7. developer.mozilla.org/en-US/docs/Web/API

CHAPTER 5

Advanced JavaScript Integration with Yew

Your journey started out with some fundamental background on what WebAssembly is and how it works. You progressed from there to build a checkers engine with nothing but your mind, a text editor, and the wast syntax.

Next, you broadened your horizons and learned how to explicitly and tightly control JavaScript interaction across the boundaries between WebAssembly and the browser's scripting host.

In this chapter, you will continue your journey away from the low-level WebAssembly syntax and learn how the combination of Rust, Rust macros, build tooling, and WebAssembly give you the power to create a complete, interactive, network-connected application written entirely in Rust and executed in the browser, maximizing code safety and performance.

Getting Started with Yew

As much as I dislike the traditional "Hello, World" program as a means to illustrate real-world lessons, I do think they have value in giving you an initial exposure to something brand new.

The *Yew* crate is unlike anything you've seen thus far in the book, and so we're going to start off with a simple example of how to build a *Yew* application before getting into the real work of building the live multi-user chat.

The samples in this chapter are written with Yew version *0.4.0*. If you're reading this book and the crates.io[1] version of Yew is up to 0.5.0 or later, you'll need to decide which version you want to use. Thanks to Cargo's excellent version pinning, the book sample written against 0.4.0 will always work as it appears in the dead tree version of this book. However, Yew 0.5.0

---

1. crates.io/crates/yew

looks like it might contain some syntax improvements as well as multi-threaded worker support. If you end up deciding to use Yew for a real application, you might want to invest some time in learning the new syntax (which is likely to include breaking changes from 0.4.0).

What Is Yew?

Inspired by the *Elm* language and the *React* JavaScript framework, Yew is a modern web application framework designed to compile to WebAssembly (wasm32-unknown-unknown), *asmjs*, or *emscripten*. We'll only be using the pure Rust WebAssembly target in this book.

Yew is a framework based on components, contexts, and message passing, creating a powerful environment for building responsive front-end applications that still operate nicely within the confines of Rust's requirements and safety constraints. It supports a virtual DOM, reusable fragments and components, and has many of the features we look for in modern JavaScript web UI frameworks.

Yew has two main Rust *traits*, which are very similar to *interfaces* in other languages. These traits are Component and Renderable. The component is responsible for providing the business logic and managing state for a discrete portion of the user interface. Anything that implements the Renderable trait is, as the name implies, responsible for producing the HTML necessary to render that entity in place within a virtual DOM. If you've had any exposure to React, then you'll recognize the power and performance benefits you get from a virtual DOM.

Yew's power comes from the use of a custom plugin build tool (which you'll install shortly), some library code, and a large number of macros in the Yew crate and others upon which it depends. It generates an enormous amount of wiring code that allows you to think in terms of pure Rust, components, and renderables, and not worry too much about how that Rust is going to work inside a browser as a WebAssembly module.

The Yew Component trait has create(), update(), change(), and destroy() functions. When you build a component you implement these functions to manage state and logic. The Yew Renderable trait simply contains the view() function, which returns HTML that should be rendered to the client.

Why Yew?

The purpose of this chapter is to show you how to build a web application using (nearly) nothing but Rust code compiled to WebAssembly. When we traditionally go to build web applications, we have to write things in JavaScript and HTML and CSS and we typically need to know a ton of frameworks on top of that (e.g., Vue, React, Angular), we need to know front-end build tools and back-end build tools, and we need to figure out where to split our code —what goes in the back end and what goes in the front end?

Frameworks like Yew let us build everything in Rust, give us the benefit of strong typing and safe code that we get from Rust, allow us to use a single, unified toolchain for our web application, and dramatically simplify the development process. Not every React application should be immediately rewritten as a "Rust-pure WebAssembly Yew" app, but hopefully by the end of the chapter, you'll have an idea of where these kinds of frameworks can come in handy. Yew is not the only web framework available for Rust and WebAssembly, but it's a mature and accessible one, so it makes for a decent book example.

As an added bonus, working with the Yew framework will expose you to some more foundational aspects of Rust, including traits, generics, referencing modules, mutable reference passing, and more.

Building Your First Yew Application

Building an application with Yew means composing a hierarchy of UI elements composed of components and renderables. The sample you'll build is a simple counter. You'll render a number and, whenever a user clicks a nearby button, the number will increase.

That might seem overly simplistic, but remember this is being done from inside Rust, built into a WebAssembly module, and then executed as JavaScript. It's worth it to take the effort to build this small sample to see how components and renderables work in Yew before moving onto a bigger problem domain. State will be maintained entirely within your Rust code, and you won't have to worry about which part of it is a back-end component and which is front-end.

The first thing you'll need to do is install Yew's required build plugin, *cargo-web*. To do that, issue the following command at a terminal prompt:

```
$ cargo install cargo-web
```

Depending on how much Rust development you've been doing on your machine, this can take quite a while for all of the components to be downloaded and compiled.

Don't confuse the cargo command with the rustup command; rustup is responsible for managing your installed toolchains and targets while cargo is responsible for building and creating your projects. For the rest of this chapter, you'll be building and running your applications with the cargo web command instead of the usual cargo.

To get started, create a new project (deleting the edition = "2018" line) with cargo new (I called mine yewcounter). Unlike previous Rust projects, you don't have to declare that the application is a dynamic library, as cargo web will take care of those details. Create a Cargo.toml that looks like this one:

yewcounter/Cargo.toml
```
[package]
name = "yewcounter"
version = "0.1.0"
authors = ["Kevin Hoffman <email@address.com"]

[dependencies]
stdweb = "0.4.2"
yew = "0.4.0"
```

The next thing we'll do is create a src/main.rs, which is typically reserved for standalone application binaries and not library modules.[2] cargo web takes care of the project metadata and compilation configuration for us, but I like being able to think of this as an *application* and not just an isolated module so the use of main.rs feels right.

In this new file, you'll see a Context structure. It implements a *trait* called AsMut. Anything that implements this trait indicates that it can expose a *mutable reference* to the type given in the generic type parameter. In this case, the context can provide a mutable reference to a *service* called ConsoleService, a service that provides access to JavaScript's console variable:

yewcounter/src/main.rs
```
extern crate yew;
extern crate yewcounter; // refers to lib.rs

use yew::prelude::*;
use yew::services::console::ConsoleService;
use yewcounter::Model;

pub struct Context {
    console: ConsoleService,
}

impl AsMut<ConsoleService> for Context {
    fn as_mut(&mut self) -> &mut ConsoleService {
        &mut self.console
    }
}
```

---

2. doc.rust-lang.org/book/ch07-00-packages-crates-and-modules.html

```
fn main() {
    yew::initialize();
    let context = Context {
        console: ConsoleService::new(),
    };
    let app: App<_, Model> = App::new(context);
    app.mount_to_body();
    yew::run_loop();
}
```

From a polymorphism perspective, the goal of what's happening with this struct and trait is the ability to pass a concrete struct type known only to the main module and have the components and renderables be able to use the services contained within that context. In other words, the UI code relies on the ability to obtain a mutable reference to a console service, but they aren't tightly coupled to *how* that service is made available. In other languages, you'd accomplish something like this with *dependency injection* or *structural typing*.

In addition to components and renderables, Yew also has the concept of services. Services, within the realm of Yew applications, are designed to expose "headless" (no UI) functionality to UI components. In this sample, the service we're using exposes the ability to log to JavaScript's console as a service. In the next sample in the chapter, you'll create a service that exposes a multi-user chat engine.

The code in the main() function is pretty standard for all Yew applications—initialize the Yew runtime, create the context that's appropriate for your application, then create an application for your *model* that takes your context as a parameter, and finally kick off the execution loop. Next, you'll define your model, which is the data read and manipulated by your component.

We'll put the model, component, and renderable in lib.rs in the same src directory as main.rs. For a more complex application, we might choose a more robust module hierarchy (you'll see some of those later in the book). In the case of a simple counter, you can express the model as just a single field on a struct:

```
pub struct Model {
    value: i64,
}
```

In keeping with the React[3]-like architecture, we need to figure out which messages (Redux developers might call them *actions*) we want to pass through

---

3.   reactjs.org/

the component to produce changes within the model, which in turn changes how the component renders. The Yew crate's stock counter sample comes with the following messages, defined by a Rust enum:

```
pub enum Msg {
    Increment,
    Decrement,
    Bulk(Vec<Msg>),
}
```

You might have noticed that one of the variants (Bulk) can actually contain a vector (array) of itself. As you'll see, this lets us bundle up multiple messages together and send them through the component as a single batch. Before getting into the full code listing for the implementation, there's some new Rust syntax to cover that you'll see:

```
impl<C> Component<C> for Model
  where
      C: AsMut<ConsoleService> {
      ...
}
```

This syntax combines Rust's generics system with its trait system. This is really one of the first areas beyond borrows, moves, and references where Rust's syntax may start to confuse people who have backgrounds in other languages. This syntax indicates that, for any instance of the Model struct, this scope contains a bound Component trait implementation when the type parameter to that component (C) implements the AsMut<ConsoleService> trait.

Putting much of the syntax details aside, this code boils down to this statement —Model can be treated *as a* Component so long as we can extract a mutable reference to a ConsoleService from the component. If you look back at the src/main.rs code, you'll see that we don't actually instantiate our Model directly. Instead, we pass it as a type parameter to Yew's App struct.

There's a similar, slightly more complex syntax that's used to define the Renderable responsible for emitting the HTML for the component:

```
impl<C> Renderable<C, Model> for Model
  where
      C: AsMut<ConsoleService> + 'static {
      ...
}
```

Essentially this code says that the Model struct can render anything that is of type Model with a context type parameter that allows us to extract a mutable reference to a ConsoleService.

I personally find this type of Rust syntax "bumpy," and it doesn't read naturally for me. The only way I learned it was simply to get used to it. Others, possibly those with more exposure to traditional C++, find this syntax more natural and low-friction. The other potentially confusing bit of syntax is the 'static bit—a *lifetime specifier*.

The Rust compiler prevents us from accessing values that may no longer exist. To do this, it needs to know how long (relatively) those values should exist. Most of the time, Rust can infer a memory lifetime and save us the bother of explicitly defining one, and it does an even better job of eliding these details in the 2018 edition syntax. But why do we need a lifetime specifier here? I'm glad you asked!

In this one line of fairly dense syntax, you can assume that the code inside the implementation block will, at some point, obtain a mutable reference to something of type ConsoleService. The Rust compiler must now police this lifetime to ensure that it lasts long enough for us to invoke the log() method on a console instance without the console instance being null due to going out of scope or being deallocated. Here, the static lifetime specifier is used. Without boring you with 20 pages of detail, this doesn't necessarily mean the value lasts forever. It just means that it has an unlimited *potential* lifetime as far as the Rust compiler is concerned. Since we know this is JavaScript's console variable, we can assume that its lifetime will never end so long as the WebAssembly module is loaded.

If you were to remove the static lifetime specifier and then try to compile the code in the upcoming listing, you'd get one of Rust's famously expressive and helpful error messages:

```
error: Could not compile `yewcounter`.

To learn more, run the command again with --verbose.
error[E0310]: the parameter type `C` may not live long enough
  --> src/lib.rs:54:9
   |
49 |    impl<C> Renderable<C, Model> for Model
   |         - help: consider adding an explicit lifetime bound `C: 'static`...
...
54 | /    html! {
55 | |      <div>
56 | |        <nav class="menu",>
57 | |          <button onclick=|_| Msg::Increment,>{ "Increment" }</button>
...  |
63 | |      </div>
64 | |    }
   | |_____^
   |
```

```
note: ...so that the type `C` will meet its required lifetime bounds
  --> src/lib.rs:54:9
   |
54 | /    html! {
55 | |        <div>
56 | |           <nav class="menu",>
57 | |              <button onclick=|_| Msg::Increment,>{ "Increment" }</button>
...|
63 | |        </div>
64 | |    }
   | |_____^
```

The error message even suggests that we should consider adding a static lifetime bound so that the C type will meet its requirements. I really do love the Rust compiler error messages—an enormous amount of community effort has gone into making them readable and provide useful hints.

Here is the completed src/lib.rs code that implements a component and a renderable for the simple counter model:

yewcounter/src/lib.rs
```rust
extern crate stdweb;
#[macro_use]
extern crate yew;

use stdweb::web::Date;
use yew::prelude::*;
use yew::services::console::ConsoleService;

pub struct Model {
    value: i64,
}

pub enum Msg {
    Increment,
    Decrement,
    Bulk(Vec<Msg>),
}

impl<C> Component<C> for Model
where
    C: AsMut<ConsoleService>,
{
    type Message = Msg;
    type Properties = ();

    fn create(_: Self::Properties, _: &mut Env<C, Self>) -> Self {
        Model { value: 0 }
    }
```

```
    fn update(&mut self, msg: Self::Message,
            env: &mut Env<C, Self>) -> ShouldRender {
        match msg {
            Msg::Increment => {
                self.value = self.value + 1;
                env.as_mut().log("plus one");
            }
            Msg::Decrement => {
                self.value = self.value - 1;
                env.as_mut().log("minus one");
            }
            Msg::Bulk(list) => for msg in list {
                self.update(msg, env);
                env.as_mut().log("Bulk action");
            },
        }
        true
    }
}

impl<C> Renderable<C, Model> for Model
where
    C: AsMut<ConsoleService> + 'static,
{
    fn view(&self) -> Html<C, Self> {
        html! {
          <div>
            <nav class="menu",>
              <button onclick=|_| Msg::Increment,>{ "Increment" }</button>
              <button onclick=|_| Msg::Decrement,>{ "Decrement" }</button>
              <button onclick=|_| Msg::Bulk(vec![Msg::Increment,
                                                 Msg::Increment]),>
                { "Increment Twice" }
              </button>
            </nav>
            <p>{ self.value }</p>
            <p>{ Date::new().to_string() }</p>
          </div>
        }
    }
}
```

The html! procedural macro (you can spot procedural macros by their exclama-
tory nature!) takes the elements contained within it and produces real HTML,
which the Yew virtual DOM will render as soon as it deems appropriate. The
html! macro is defined by the stdweb[4] crate, along with the js! macro that will emit
in-situ JavaScript wherever encountered in your Rust code.

---

4.   crates.io/crates/stdweb

Pay close attention to what's inside the html! macro, though. It might look like regular HTML, but it's really just tokens waiting to be parsed by Rust. As such, you'll notice that the macro requires a comma after every attribute=value segment, even if it precedes the closing markup character. It takes a little getting used to, and readers with experience using React's JSX have seen this kind of mild frustration before. If you're using a text editor with real Rust support, though, it should be able to detect syntax errors in your macro and try to warn you (though the error message may often seem obscure).

With these two files written, it's time to compile and run this application. If you're wondering where the index.js JavaScript file is or the index.html file is— we don't need them. At least, not for this sample because Yew builds some reasonable defaults for us via cargo web:

```
$ cargo web build --target=wasm32-unknown-unknown
   Compiling yewcounter v0.1.0
(file:///home/kevin/Code/Rust/wasmbook/khrust/Book/code/yewcounter)
    Finished release [optimized] target(s) in 0.19s
   Compiling yewcounter v0.1.0
(file:///home/kevin/Code/Rust/wasmbook/khrust/Book/code/yewcounter)
    Finished release [optimized] target(s) in 3.57s
    Processing "yewcounter.wasm"...
    Finished processing of "yewcounter.wasm"!
$ cargo web start --target=wasm32-unknown-unknown
    Finished release [optimized] target(s) in 0.04s
    Processing "yewcounter.wasm"...
    Finished processing of "yewcounter.wasm"!
```

```
If you need to serve any extra files, put them in the 'static' directory
in the root of your crate. They'll be served alongside your application.
You can also put a 'static' directory in your 'src' directory.

Your application is being served at '/yewcounter.js'. It will be automatically
rebuilt if you make any changes in your code.

You can access the web server at `http://[::1]:8000`.
```

Let's open the indicated website and see what we get:

Playing with this application feels just like it would if you had written it entirely in JavaScript—clicking the buttons provides immediate feedback. You can also see the invocations of the console service by checking the JavaScript console. And you can see that the invocations are happening inside yewcounter.js, a file generated completely on your behalf by the Yew build tool:

```
Finished loading Rust wasm module 'yewcounter'
plus one
minus one
plus one
Bulk action
```

Now that you've seen the basics behind building a service, a component, and a renderable in Yew, let's build on that knowledge by creating a multi-user chat application sitting on top of a third-party JavaScript chat engine.

Building a Live Chat Application

Building on some basic exposure to the *Yew* programming model, it's time to create something a bit more complex and powerful than an app that increments a counter. You've got the basic building blocks already: components, renderables, and services—the trick lies in figuring out where and how to stack those blocks.

For this next sample, we're going to stack the building blocks to make a real-time chat application. This app will have an area that displays chat messages, an area that shows the currently online users, and an area that lets you enter your alias and connect.

Luckily we won't have to do all the multi-user, real-time chat work ourselves. There are companies and products that can help here, including Pubnub, Ably, XMPP platforms, Rapid.io, Emitter.io, and the list goes on *ad infinitum*.

Due to its ease of use and the fact that one does not have to supply a credit card number to begin experimenting, I've decided to use Pubnub's *ChatEngine* product to provide the underlying infrastructure for this WebAssembly app. If you have concerns about signing up for this service, feel free to read along without doing so or simply supply minimal information and delete your account when you're done with the samples.

Creating a Pubnub Account and Keys

If you don't already have your free Pubnub account, head on over to their home page[5] and create one. You'll need to provide some basic information,

---

5.   www.pubnub.com

but it's a five-minute process that goes even faster if you want to authenticate using a Google ID (again, for the security-conscious, you can skip using your Google ID and create new credentials instead)

After signing up and getting to your main dashboard, you'll see tiles for each of your applications. You'll be creating an application for this sample, but don't create a new one with the "Create New app" button. Instead, if you see a banner advertising the ChatEngine product at the top, click that link. If you don't see it, then you can manually go to the ChatEngine tutorial page.[6]

Once at the tutorial/quick-start, you should see a button called Setup, like the one in the screenshot from Pubnub's website:

What is ChatEngine?

ChatEngine makes it easy to build powerful, cross-platform chat on PubNub. It provides essential components (messages, users, typing indicators), microservices infrastructure (chatbots and programmability) and the network to build and scale production-ready chat apps.

Quickstart Overview

This quickstart will walk you through building a basic chat app with ChatEngine. We'll use vanilla JavaScript, but worry not, ChatEngine supports iOS and Android as well.

All the functional code is provided here via Codepen.

1. **Configure Your Account**

   First, configure your account for ChatEngine and get your publish/subscribe keys. Start by creating an account and activating ChatEngine:

   Setup

When you click the setup button, Pubnub will create an application for you, but it will also create a *function* in your application that hosts your chat engine server. This function being up and running is the essential key to being able to use the ChatEngine functionality. If you navigate to the functions button and then click on your ChatEngine function, you should see a screen like the one shown in the figure on page 101.

If the function isn't running, start it now. If the navigation doesn't match what I've described in the book, then Pubnub may have changed their design and you might need to search around in their new interface to find out how to get set up. Before heading to the next section, you'll need to know the

---

6. www.pubnub.com/tutorials/chatengine/

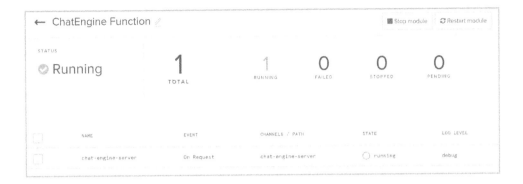

publish and subscribe keys for your app and be sure that your ChatEngine function is running.

The goal of this chapter isn't to write a *Pubnub* app, it's to illustrate how you can wrap third-party JavaScript libraries inside your own Rust WebAssembly modules and utilize auto-generated bridge code to communicate between your Rust/Yew code and another JavaScript library that you don't own.

Building a Yew Service for Pubnub

Yew services are blocks of functionality that can be exposed to renderables and components. They're designed specifically to act as gateways (or facades or *Anti-Corruption Layers* depending on which terminology is your favorite) between your code and other dependencies.

In this case, the dependency is a JavaScript library from Pubnub. Because we're using Yew and building on top of other code generation tools that make interacting with JavaScript easy, it should be fairly straightforward to wrap some of the functions in the ChatEngine module as a Yew service. Of course, "fairly straightforward" is usually how all innocent endeavors appear until they explode in a fiery ball. There are a couple of quirks to watch out for here.

The largest quirk here is one that caused me endless hours of frustration involving a conflict between my own code, asynchronous JavaScript, and my own JS inexperience. I had two options: either force synchronous operations and wait for manual initialization to finish, or declare a global variable (myChat) to hold the handle to the chat conversation once the futures completed.

I chose the latter, which required me to add a couple of JavaScript variables to the top of the index.html shown here. Those with better JavaScript chops than I might want to refactor these global variables out as an exercise to get more familiar with Yew+JavaScript interaction subtleties. Try capturing the third-party library variables inside a Yew service, if you can:

```
yew_wasmchat/static/index.html
<!doctype html>
<html lang="en">

<head>
  <meta charset="utf-8">
  <title>Yew • Online Chat</title>
  <link rel="stylesheet" href="styles.css">
  <script
    src="https://cdn.jsdelivr.net/npm/chat-engine@0.9.18/
        dist/chat-engine.min.js"
    type="text/javascript">
  </script>
  <link
    rel="stylesheet"
    type="text/css"
    href="https://maxcdn.bootstrapcdn.com/font-awesome/
        4.4.0/css/font-awesome.min.css">
  </link>
</head>

<body>
  <script id="bootstrap">
    var myChat;
    var me;
  </script>
  <script src="js/app.js"></script>
</body>

</html>
```

To get started with this project, you can copy the counter project from earlier.
I put mine in a directory called yew_wasmchat. The first changes you'll need to
make will be to Cargo.toml to add a few new dependencies:

```
yew_wasmchat/Cargo.toml
[package]
name = "wasmchat"
version = "0.1.0"
authors = ["Kevin Hoffman <your@address.com>"]

[dependencies]
web_logger = "0.1"
log = "0.4"
strum = "0.9"
strum_macros = "0.9"
serde = "1"
serde_json = "1"
serde_derive = "1"
stdweb = "0.4.8"
yew = "0.4.0"
```

Web Logger is a handy little crate. Once initialized, web_logger will allow all of your Rust-native log macros (info!, debug!, etc.) to generate very nice log messages in the JavaScript console. You wrote a small wrapper around console.log earlier in the book—this is just a fancier version of that same concept bundled as a crate. The serde dependencies all deal with serialization and de-serialization.

There will be three files in this project: src/lib.rs, src/main.rs, and src/services.rs. The initialization takes place in main.rs, lib.rs contains the UI, and services.rs contains our Pubnub wrapper.

Let's take a look at the service implementation and then step through some of the parts that might look a little crazy:

```
yew_wasmchat/src/services.rs
use super::Message;
use stdweb::Value;
use yew::prelude::*;

pub struct PubnubService {
    lib: Option<Value>,
    chat: Option<Value>,
}

impl PubnubService {
    pub fn new(publish_key: &str, subscribe_key: &str) -> Self {
        info!("Creating new instance of pubnub chatengine service");
        let chat_engine = js! {
            let ce = ChatEngineCore.create({
                publishKey: @{publish_key},
                subscribeKey: @{subscribe_key}
            });
            console.log("Chat engine core created");
            return ce;
        };
        PubnubService {
            lib: Some(chat_engine),
            chat: None,
        }
    }

    pub fn send_message(&mut self, msg: &str) -> () {
        js! {
            let m = @{msg};
            myChat.emit("message", {
                text: m
            });
        }
    }
}
```
❶

❷

```rust
pub fn connect(
    &mut self,
    topic: &str,
    nickname: &str,
    onmessage: Callback<Message>,
    onoffline: Callback<String>,
    ononline: Callback<String>,
) -> () {
    let lib = self.lib.as_ref().expect("No pubnub library!");

    let chat_callback = move |text: String, source: String| {
        let msg = Message {
            text: text,
            from: source,
        };
        onmessage.emit(msg);
    };

    let useroffline_callback = move |username: String| {
        onoffline.emit(username);
    };

    let useronline_callback = move |username: String| {
        ononline.emit(username);
    };

    let chat = js! {
        var pn = @{lib};
        var chat_callback = @{chat_callback};
        var online_cb = @{useronline_callback};
        var offline_cb = @{useroffline_callback};

        pn.on("$.ready", function(data) {
            console.log("PubNub Chat Engine Ready");
            // set global variable
            me = data.me;
            // create a new ChatEngine Chat (global var)
            myChat = new pn.Chat(@{topic});

            myChat.on("$.connected", () => {
                console.log("The chat is connected!");

                myChat.on("message", (message) => {
                    chat_callback(message.data.text,
                                  message.sender.state.nickName);
                    console.log("message: " + message.data.text +
                        " from " + message.sender.state.nickName);
                });
                myChat.on("$.online.*", (data) => {
                    console.log("User is Online: ", data.user);
                    online_cb(data.user.state.nickName);
                });
```

```
                    myChat.on("$.offline.*", (data) => {
                        console.log("User is Offline: ", data.user);
                        offline_cb(data.user.state.nickName);
                    });
                });
            });
            pn.connect(String(new Date().getTime()), {
                nickName: @{nickname}
            });

            console.log("pubnub connecting");
            return myChat;
        };
        self.chat = Some(chat);
    }
}
```

❶ Inject JavaScript to instantiate Pubnub's ChatEnginecore.

❷ Return a new PubnubService with a captured reference to the chat engine JavaScript object.

❸ Define a set of callback functions that will be invoked by various Chat Engine handlers.

❹ Inject the JavaScript necessary to attach the Rust/wasm callbacks to chat engine JavaScript handlers.

Let's take a closer look at this bit of code from the PubnubService::new() function:

```
let chat_engine = js! {
    let ce = ChatEngineCore.create({
        publishKey: @{publish_key},
        subscribeKey: @{subscribe_key}
    });
    console.log("Chat engine core created");
    return ce;
};
```

There's a lot happening that you *don't see*, so let's walk through everything that's happening in detail:

- Everything inside the js! block is wrapped in a private scope and converted into a JavaScript function that shows up in the generated JavaScript file.

- The publish_key and subscribe_key parameters are made available as function parameters in this JavaScript snippet.

- An extern block is created for this anonymous JavaScript function to allow it to be invoked from WebAssembly.

- The "pass as a string" pattern is used to allow these values to be passed to the JavaScript function by way of shared linear memory.

- At runtime, this anonymous function is invoked. The return value is stored as an object reference in linear memory.

- That object reference is handed to Rust as a return value and stored in chat_engine.

This is what is involved with just a few lines of js! macro, and that is even with a few of the gory details being glossed over here to try to keep things easy to follow. Hopefully, after having spent a few chapters doing things the hard way, you are better able to follow the amount of work macros like this save you.

Now you've seen what it looks like when you want to execute some JavaScript that captures data via closure around Rust lexically scoped values and then stores the return value of that JavaScript block as a native Rust variable. I think it's worth it to take a moment, pause, and thank the code generation gremlins for their assistance here, recognizing how much power is now at your fingertips.

Creating the Yew Chat UI

The user interface for the chat application is fairly simple. There's an area for messages that come from the chat engine (via the PubnubService), an area that shows the list of connected users, an area that lets us provide an alias and connect, and lastly, a textbox that lets us type text that will be transmitted to all other users when we hit Enter.

To reproduce this layout, you can find both the index.html and styles.css files in the static directory in the code sample download for the book.

As you now know, a Yew UI is composed of components, renderables, and messages that are used to trigger updates. This app will have the following messages:

- SendChat - indicates a text message should be sent out through the chat engine

- AddMessage - indicates that we should add a text message to a component's internal state

- Connect - performs a chat engine connection via the service

- EnterName - occurs as the user types in the "name" textbox
- UserOnline - indication of a change in presence status from the chat engine service
- UserOffline - indication of a change in presence status from the chat engine service
- UpdatePendingText - occurs as the user types in the text input box for the outbound chat message

We're going to create a component to manage state and we're going to create a renderable to manage the HTML output and virtual DOM manipulation. In the following component code, the create() function is called to initialize state, while its update() function is called every time a message bubbles up through the queue. Most of the time, messages make their way to the update() function by virtue of event handlers in renderables.

Note that the Msg type is used for Yew component internal messaging and the Message type represents the data for a chat message. We use env.send_back() to dispatch a Msg:

```
yew_wasmchat/src/lib.rs
#![recursion_limit = "512"]

extern crate strum;
#[macro_use]
extern crate serde_derive;
#[macro_use]
extern crate yew;
#[macro_use]
extern crate log;

#[macro_use]
extern crate stdweb;

use services::PubnubService;
use std::collections::HashSet;
use yew::prelude::*;

#[derive(Serialize, Deserialize, Debug)]
pub struct Message {
    pub text: String,
    pub from: String,
}

pub struct Model {
    alias: String,
    pending_text: String,
    messages: Vec<Message>,
    users: HashSet<String>,
}
```

```rust
#[derive(Debug)]
pub enum Msg {
    SendChat,
    AddMessage(Message),
    Connect,
    EnterName(String),
    UserOffline(String),
    UserOnline(String),
    UpdatePendingText(String),
    NoOp,
}

impl<C> Component<C> for Model
where
    C: AsMut<PubnubService> + 'static,
{
    type Message = Msg;
    type Properties = ();

    fn create(_: Self::Properties, _: &mut Env<C, Self>) -> Self {
        Model {
            messages: Vec::new(),
            alias: "".into(),
            users: HashSet::new(),
            pending_text: "".into(),
        }
    }

    fn update(&mut self, msg: Self::Message,
            env: &mut Env<C, Self>) -> ShouldRender {
        match msg {
            Msg::AddMessage(msg) => {
                self.messages.push(msg);
            }
            Msg::UserOnline(nick) => {
                info!("Adding user {:?}", nick);
                self.users.insert(nick);
            }
            Msg::UserOffline(nick) => {
                info!("Removing user {:?}", nick);
                self.users.remove(&nick);
            }
            Msg::SendChat => {
                info!("Called send chat!");
                env.as_mut().send_message(&self.pending_text);
                self.pending_text = "".into();
            }
            Msg::Connect => {
                let on_message = env.send_back(|msg| Msg::AddMessage(msg));
                let onoffline = env.send_back(|user| Msg::UserOffline(user));
                let ononline = env.send_back(|user| Msg::UserOnline(user));
```

```
            env.as_mut().connect(
                "chatengine-demo-chat",
                &self.alias,
                on_message,
                onoffline,
                ononline,
            );
        }
        Msg::EnterName(n) => {
            self.alias = n;
        }
        Msg::UpdatePendingText(s) => {
            self.pending_text = s;
        }
        Msg::NoOp => {}
    }
    true
    }
}
```

Now that we have a component complete with message dispatching and state management, let's create the renderable view for this component:

```
yew_wasmchat/src/lib.rs
impl<C> Renderable<C, Model> for Model
where
    C: AsMut<PubnubService> + 'static,
{
    fn view(&self) -> Html<C, Self> {
        html! {
        <div class="wrapper",>
          <div class="chat-text",>
            <h1>{ "Messages" }</h1><br/>
            <ul class="message-list",>
              { for self.messages.iter().enumerate().map(view_message) }
            </ul>
          </div>
          <div class="users",>
            <h1>{ "Users" }</h1><br/>
            <ul class="user-list",>
              { for self.users.iter().enumerate().map(view_user) }
            </ul>
          </div>
          <div class="connect",>
            <input placeholder="Your Name",
              value=&self.alias,
              oninput=|e| Msg::EnterName(e.value),>
            </input>
            <button onclick=|_| Msg::Connect,>{ "Connect" }</button>
          </div>
```

```
            <div class="text-entry",>
              <input placeholder="Message Text",
                class="pending-text",
                value=&self.pending_text,
                oninput=|e| Msg::UpdatePendingText(e.value),
                onkeypress=|e| {
                  if e.key() == "Enter" { Msg::SendChat } else { Msg::NoOp }
                },>
              </input>
            </div>
          </div>
          }
        }
    }
}
```

Keep an eye on the code inside the html! macro. As you experiment with this and try to add more controls, you will undoubtedly produce a syntax error and the error message might not be immediately obvious because it's a parse failure rather than a language syntax error.

Inside the view() function, there are some utility functions that let us abstract out and potentially reuse views: view_message() and view_user(). They each take a tuple as a parameter and return HTML snippets:

```
yew_wasmchat/src/lib.rs
fn view_message<C>((_idx, message): (usize, &Message)) -> Html<C, Model>
where
    C: AsMut<PubnubService> + 'static,
{
    html! {
      <li>
        <label>
          <span class="sender",>{"["}{&message.from}{"]"}</span>
          <span class="chatmsg",>{&message.text}</span>
        </label>
      </li>
    }
}

fn view_user<C>((_idx, user): (usize, &String)) -> Html<C, Model>
where
    C: AsMut<PubnubService> + 'static,
{
    html! {
      <li>
        <label>{ user }</label>
      </li>
    }
}

pub mod services;
```

Finally, now that you've got a chat engine service sitting on top of a valid, active *Pubnub* account, you can create a src/main.rs to initialize the application and components:

yew_wasmchat/src/main.rs
```rust
extern crate wasmchat;
extern crate web_logger;
extern crate yew;

use wasmchat::{services::PubnubService, Model};
use yew::prelude::*;

pub struct Context {
    pubnub: PubnubService,
}

impl AsMut<PubnubService> for Context {
    fn as_mut(&mut self) -> &mut PubnubService {
        &mut self.pubnub
    }
}

fn main() {
    web_logger::init();
    yew::initialize();

    let context = Context {
        pubnub: PubnubService::new("(your publish key)",
                                   "(your subscribe key)"),
    };

    let app: App<_, Model> = App::new(context);
    app.mount_to_body();
    yew::run_loop();
}
```

Make sure that you replace the publish and subscribe keys with the ones you got from your own application. Run the following commands from the project root (the same directory as Cargo.toml):

```
$ cargo web build --target=wasm32-unknown-unknown
    Processing "wasmchat.wasm"...
    Finished processing of "wasmchat.wasm"!
$ cargo web start --target=wasm32-unknown-unknown
    Processing "wasmchat.wasm"...
    Finished processing of "wasmchat.wasm"!

If you need to serve any extra files, put them in the 'static' directory
in the root of your crate. They'll be served alongside your application.
You can also put a 'static' directory in your 'src' directory.

Your application is being served at '/wasmchat.js'. It will automatically
rebuild if you make any changes in your code.

You can access the web server at `http://[::1]:8000`.
```

You should be able to open this application in two separate tabs, provide two aliases, and hit the Connect button. You can then have an intense and thought-provoking discussion with yourself as shown in this screenshot:

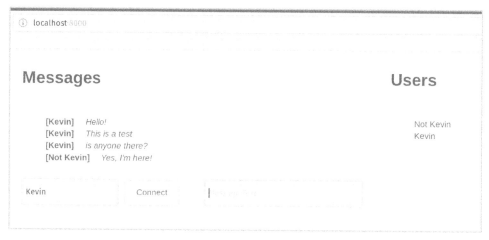

Wrapping Up

It's been a long journey since the early days when you were building checkers games with raw wast. You've seen the underpinnings of WebAssembly and its architecture, you've learned how to write low-level code, how to interact with JavaScript via manual extern blocks, and in this chapter you took advantage of libraries and code generation to build a nearly 100% Rust WebAssembly application that even uses a third-party chat engine.

Your Jedi training in JavaScript integration is complete. You must now move on and learn new, more powerful techniques. In the coming chapters, you will experiment with hosting WebAssembly modules in Rust applications rather than the browser. You'll extrapolate from what you've learned about JavaScript integration to build WebAssembly modules that run on Raspberry Pis or that can even battle each other in online multiplayer combat.

Part III

Working with Non-Web Hosts

Let's take our WebAssembly skills to the next level and explore some exciting use cases for hosting WebAssembly modules in Rust applications.

CHAPTER 6

Hosting Modules Outside the Browser

Now that you've learned the ins and outs of creating WebAssembly modules with the wast syntax and with Rust, and you've learned how a web browser provides the necessary functionality to host WebAssembly modules, it's time to take that knowledge to the next level: Rust hosting.

At the very beginning of the book, I asked you to trust me when I told you WebAssembly was about more than just the web—it was about creating portable modules that could be slotted into all kinds of hosts, not just browsers.

In this chapter, I'll make good on that promise and show you how to write Rust code that performs the same job as a web browser in order to host WebAssembly modules. You'll see how to load, interpret, and execute those modules as well as how to provide callable host functions and to take advantage of functions and memory exported from a WebAssembly module. By the end of the chapter, you'll be able to build a console application that can load checkers modules and interactively play them, all without even a hint of the Internet or a web browser.

How to Be a Good Host

So far, you've seen what the browser does for WebAssembly modules, and you probably have a good instinct for what tasks the browser is performing. But I haven't yet been explicit about the things a host needs to do in order to play nice in the WebAssembly ecosystem.

WebAssembly specifies a mutual contract between the module and the host responsible for it. This contract details the things that the host must provide to the module, the things the module must provide to the host, as well as other assertions that are required to "make the magic happen." As you'll see, the terms of this contract are what allow WebAssembly to be so portable, and to work in or out of a web browser—a characteristic that sets this technology apart from so many of its predecessors.

To be a good host, you need to ensure that you do all of the following:

Load and Validate the wasm Binary

The binary wasm file format is a well-documented specification. Any application acting as a host is responsible for loading the bytes from that file and validating that all of the preconditions for the raw format of the file are correct. This doesn't validate behavior, only that the file itself is valid. This may seem obvious, but it has a number of important implications, including the inability for a WebAssembly module to bootstrap its own execution and thus become an attack vector.

Expose Exports

Every WebAssembly module has to have at least one function export. Otherwise, the host can do nothing with it. Each host is responsible for going through the list of exported functions, linear memory, and so on, and choosing how to deal with that. For functions, the host is responsible for providing the bridge "glue" that allows a function invocation from the host to execute the appropriate function in the WebAssembly module.

Satisfy Imports

In addition to exporting things for the host to use, WebAssembly modules can also import things that must be satisfied by the host, like functions and linear memory. There is some flexibility in the *how* and *when*, but every host needs to be able to validate that the demands made by the module imports can be met, and if not, providing an appropriate error to the host-based code.

Interpret (execute) the Module

Once asked to invoke a WebAssembly function, the host is responsible for traversing through the list of instructions (the numeric/opcode versions of the instructions you saw when you wrote wast by hand earlier in the book), maintaining state, and handling errors. If a module has a start() function, the host needs to at least offer the option to execute that so the module can initialize itself.

Module Isolation

The host is responsible for properly isolating modules. They shouldn't be able to talk to each other or view or modify any data without going through the proper channels. There is nothing preventing a host from allowing exported memory from one module to be imported by another module. Whether or not to allow this sort of behavior is entirely up to the host. A module failure should never be able to crash another module, nor should it be possible to execute un-exported (private) functions or see private data.

Now that we know the rules for being a good host, let's go build one in Rust.

Interpreting WebAssembly Modules with Rust

If we really enjoyed punishing ourselves with loads of tedious work, we could start with the binary interface and write a parser for it. We could then write code that maintains the stack state, executes the various WebAssembly core instructions, and manages linear memory and all the other things needed for the low-level interface.

Thankfully we don't have to do that. The creators of the wasmi[1] crate have done us a huge favor in that regard. Originally designed as a way to help Parity Tech create an ethereum client for contracts implemented in WebAssembly, Parity pulled the core pieces out of their code and made separate crates for interpreting and manipulating WebAssembly modules.

You'll get your first exposure to this crate by accomplishing the simplest task —executing a WebAssembly function in a module that has no import needs and exports nothing but a single function. To get started, create a new binary Rust project with the following command:

```
$ cargo new --bin wasmi_add
```

This creates a new Rust project that is a standalone binary (we've been creating dynamic libraries for WebAssembly modules so far) that can be executed from the command line. The first step is to add a dependency on the wasmi crate to the project:

```
wasmi_add/Cargo.toml
[package]
name = "wasmi_add"
version = "0.1.0"
authors = ["Your Address <you@address.com>"]

[dependencies]
wasmi = "0.4.0"
```

Replace your default main.rs with the following code. We'll be adding to it piece by piece as this code is probably new, even to many veteran Rust program-mers. In the first section, our main() function returns a Result type. This lets us use the ? operation that will either give us the good value inside the result or return an error from the function immediately.

---

1.   github.com/paritytech/wasmi

The first thing you'll do is load the WebAssembly module from the fundamentals chapter (add.wasm) into a vector of bytes (the u8 type) and create a Module from that buffer:

wasmi_add/src/main.rs
```
extern crate wasmi;

use std::error::Error;
use std::fs::File;
use std::io::Read;
use wasmi::{ImportsBuilder, ModuleInstance, NopExternals, RuntimeValue};

fn main() -> Result<(), Box<Error>> {
    let mut buffer = Vec::new();
    {
        let mut f = File::open("../fundamentals/add.wasm")?;
        f.read_to_end(&mut buffer)?;
    }
    let module = wasmi::Module::from_buffer(buffer)?;
```

Next, we'll create an *instance* of the module. You can think of this as a "running copy" of the module, which has its own state, memory, etc. As a host, the module instance is what you'll interact with most of the time:

wasmi_add/src/main.rs
```
let instance = ModuleInstance::new(&module, &ImportsBuilder::default())
    .expect("Failed to instantiate WASM module")
    .assert_no_start();
```

This code creates a new module with a default set of imports, meaning we're not satisfying any imports demanded by the module yet. The assert_no_start() function gives us an executable module instance that will panic if the module has a start() function. If we knew our module needed initialization, we'd call the run_start() function instead. The use of expect() is just another way of forcing a panic if we get a failing result.

Now that we've got a module instance, we can invoke a function. As a refresher, here's what our add() function looked like:

```
(module
  (func $add (param $lhs i32) (param $rhs i32) (result i32)
    (i32.add
        (get_local $lhs)
        (get_local $rhs)
    )
  )
  (export "add" (func $add))
)
```

This code takes two i32 parameters and returns an i32 value. We execute that using the wasmi crate like so:

```
wasmi_add/src/main.rs
let mut args = Vec::<RuntimeValue>::new();
args.push(RuntimeValue::from(42));
args.push(RuntimeValue::from(1));

let result: Option<RuntimeValue> =
    instance.invoke_export("add", &args, &mut NopExternals)?;
```

Here you call invoke_export() with the name of the exported function. This name *must* match and is case-sensitive. The RuntimeValue is used as a way of converting from Rust-native data types into values that can be passed onto the WebAssembly stack as function parameters. It's an enum, and as such, it's incredibly easy to use pattern matching to extract results from, as shown in the rest of the code from main.rs:

```
wasmi_add/src/main.rs
    match result {
        Some(RuntimeValue::I32(v)) => {
            println!("The answer to your addition was {}", v);
        }
        Some(_) => {
            println!("Got a value of an unexpected data type");
        }
        None => {
            println!("Failed to get a result from wasm invocation");
        }
    }
    Ok(())
}
```

There are a couple of places in this code that are more verbose than they needed to be, but it helps to see how everything works in long form before taking some shortcuts. When you run this code, you should see that it performs the addition just the way you'd expect:

```
$ cargo run
  Compiling wasmi_add v0.1.0
    (file:///home/kevin/Code/Rust/wasmbook/khrust/Book/code/wasmi_add)
  Finished dev [unoptimized + debuginfo] target(s) in 1.48s
  Running `target/debug/wasmi_add`
The answer to your addition was 43
```

And just like that, you've created a Rust console application that hosts a WebAssembly module. Hopefully the real power of WebAssembly is starting to hit you. Because next, we're going to build a Rust console application that can run the checkers game we wrote earlier in the book.

Building a Console Host Checkers Player

As exciting as it may have been to be able to invoke the add() function in one of our earlier WebAssembly modules, eventually writing all of that low-level code is going to feel tedious. As a result, a pattern starts to emerge when we create Rust hosts for WebAssembly modules. This pattern involves:

Creating an Imports Resolver

In wasmi terms, this is an implementation of the ModuleImportResolver trait. Its job is to provide a signature and numeric invocation index for each function imported by the module.

Creating a Runtime for Externals

Each time the host invokes a module function, it has to pass something that implements the Externals trait. This is typically referred to as the *runtime*, and it's what allows the module to invoke imported functions.

Creating an API Wrapper for Exported Functions

Manual invocations of WebAssembly module functions is tedious and just feels very clumsy and stiff compared to idiomatic Rust. So, when we are hosting a WebAssembly module, we can create a wrapper API around it for the same reason that wasm-bindgen does when it builds a JavaScript wrapper file.

We'll be walking through each of these steps individually as we build the checkers host. But first, create a new Rust binary project called wasmi_checkers and add the wasmi dependency to it.

Resolving Imports

Import resolution is done *callback style*. As the wasmi system goes through the module to create a running instance, it sifts through the list of imports in a module. For each one of those imports, it will call the resolve_func() on the import resolver that we've specified during the module instantiation.

This function is responsible for turning the name of the import (remember, case-sensitive) into an instance of something that can then be used for function invocation. This is the wasmi type FuncRef, which is built by supplying a *function index* and some metadata about the function signature. If the signature we provide as a host doesn't match the signature defined in the module, we can return an error and stop execution.

Our checkers module had two imports that needed to be provided by the host: *piecemoved* and *piececrowned*. These imports were in the *events* scope or namespace. To refresh your memory, here's the declaration of those imports from the original code:

```
(import "events" "piecemoved"
  (func $notify_piecemoved (param $fromX i32) (param $fromY i32)
                           (param $toX i32) (param $toY i32)))
(import "events" "piececrowned"
  (func $notify_piececrowned (param $pieceX i32) (param $pieceY i32)))
```

To build a resolver that handles these, create a new file called imports.rs in the same directory as your main.rs. Add the following code:

```
wasmi_checkers/src/imports.rs
use wasmi::{
    Error as InterpreterError, FuncInstance,
    FuncRef, ModuleImportResolver, Signature, ValueType,
};

pub const PIECEMOVED_INDEX: usize = 0;
pub const PIECECROWNED_INDEX: usize = 1;

pub struct RuntimeModuleImportResolver;

impl RuntimeModuleImportResolver {
    pub fn new() -> RuntimeModuleImportResolver {
        RuntimeModuleImportResolver {}
    }
}

impl<'a> ModuleImportResolver for RuntimeModuleImportResolver {
    fn resolve_func(
        &self,
        field_name: &str,
        _signature: &Signature,
    ) -> Result<FuncRef, InterpreterError> {
        let func_ref = match field_name {
```
❶
```
            "piecemoved" => FuncInstance::alloc_host(
                Signature::new(
                    &[
                        ValueType::I32,
                        ValueType::I32,
                        ValueType::I32,
                        ValueType::I32,
                    ][..],
                    None,
                ),
                PIECEMOVED_INDEX,
            ),
```
❷
```
            "piececrowned" => FuncInstance::alloc_host(
                Signature::new(&[ValueType::I32, ValueType::I32][..], None),
                PIECECROWNED_INDEX,
            ),
            _ => {
```

```
❸                  return Err(InterpreterError::Function(format!(
                       "host module doesn't export function with name {}",
                       field_name
                   )))
               }
           };
           Ok(func_ref)
       }
   }
```

❶ Provide a FuncRef for the piecemoved() function.

❷ Provide a FuncRef for the piececrowned() function.

❸ Return an error if the module is trying to import a function we don't know about.

Where the import resolver is all about assigning numeric indexes and metadata to imported functions, the runtime performs the actual execution, as you'll see next.

Satisfying Externals with a Runtime

The complement to the resolve_func() function is the invoke_index() function, called on an implementation of the Externals trait. This central function operates like a dispatcher, and it's our job to pull out the arguments, analyze the function index, and decide what to invoke and how to invoke it.

It's a pretty good choice to have the target of your dispatch function be on the same anchor struct. That way, in case your runtime host needs to maintain its own state, it can make that state available to the functions being called by the module. This also helps ensure that data correlated to each module is isolated from other modules you might be running in memory. Add the runtime.rs file to your src directory and place the following code in it:

wasmi_checkers/src/runtime.rs
```
use super::imports::{PIECECROWNED_INDEX, PIECEMOVED_INDEX};

use wasmi::{Externals, RuntimeArgs, RuntimeValue, Trap};

❶ pub struct Runtime {}

impl Runtime {
    pub fn new() -> Runtime {
        Runtime {}
    }

❷  fn handle_piece_moved(
        &self,
        from: (i32, i32),
        to: (i32, i32),
```

```
        ) -> Result<Option<RuntimeValue>, Trap> {
            println!(
                "A piece was moved from ({},{}) to ({},{})",
                from.0, from.1, to.0, to.1
            );
            Ok(None)
        }

❸      fn handle_piece_crowned(
            &self,
            loc: (i32, i32)) -> Result<Option<RuntimeValue>, Trap> {
            println!("A piece was crowned at ({},{})", loc.0, loc.1);
            Ok(None)
        }
    }

    impl Externals for Runtime {
❹      fn invoke_index(
            &mut self,
            index: usize,
            args: RuntimeArgs,
        ) -> Result<Option<RuntimeValue>, Trap> {
            match index {
                PIECECROWNED_INDEX => {
                    let piece_x: i32 = args.nth(0);
                    let piece_y: i32 = args.nth(1);
                    self.handle_piece_crowned((piece_x, piece_y))
                }
                PIECEMOVED_INDEX => {
                    let from_x: i32 = args.nth(0);
                    let from_y: i32 = args.nth(1);
                    let to_x: i32 = args.nth(2);
                    let to_y: i32 = args.nth(3);
                    self.handle_piece_moved((from_x, from_y), (to_x, to_y))
                }
                _ => panic!("unknown function index"),
            }
        }
    }
}
```

❶ Great place to put module-specific state

❷ Dispatcher calls this function when appropriate

❸ Dispatcher calls this function when appropriate

❹ Central dispatcher, converts function index to call result

We now have a checkers runtime and a checkers import resolver. The two of these things can be encapsulated within a single checkers API that hides all of the wasmi implementation details and can even hide the presence of WebAssembly entirely. We'll build such an API next.

> ## Module State
>
> Perhaps you're wondering why we would want to maintain our own state for a module when, as we know, the module is capable of maintaining its own state via linear memory. Host state bound to a particular module comes in handy when we want to maintain data that we don't want the module to manipulate directly.
>
> For example, we could maintain the *health* or *hit points* of the entity controlled by a WebAssembly module, and we don't want the module to cheat by having direct access to that state. We could also maintain a win/loss count for a checkers module, etc.

Creating the Checkers Game API

There's one last thing to do before we can use Rust to host our checkers WebAssembly module—build an API layer. We don't want to expose to the consumer of the checkers game all of the low-level details of how to interface with WebAssembly modules. If we wanted, we could even try to hide the existence of the wasm file itself. But in this case, we want syntax like Checkers-Game::new("/path/to/file.wasm").

To do this, create a checkersgame.rs file in the src directory of your project. Add this initial bit of code to the file to create a function that encapsulates the logic to read the file from disk and create a module instance from it:

```
wasmi_checkers/src/checkersgame.rs
use std::error::Error;
use std::fs::File;
use std::io::prelude::*;
use wasmi::{
    ExternVal, ImportsBuilder, MemoryRef, Module,
    ModuleImportResolver, ModuleInstance, ModuleRef, RuntimeValue,
};

use super::imports::RuntimeModuleImportResolver;
use super::runtime::Runtime;

pub struct CheckersGame {
    runtime: Runtime,
    module_instance: ModuleRef,
}

#[derive(Debug)]
pub enum PieceColor {
    White,
    Black,
}

type Result<T> = ::std::result::Result<T, Box<Error>>;
type Coordinate = (i32, i32);
```

```
fn load_instance(import_resolver: &impl ModuleImportResolver,
                 module_file: &str) -> Result<ModuleRef>
{
    let mut buffer = Vec::new();
    let mut f = File::open(module_file)?;
    f.read_to_end(&mut buffer)?;
    let module = Module::from_buffer(buffer)?;
    let mut builder = ImportsBuilder::new();
    builder.push_resolver("events", import_resolver);

    Ok(ModuleInstance::new(&module, &builder)
        .expect("Failed to instantiate WASM module")
        .assert_no_start())
}
```

There's a little bit of Rust generics in here, but it's not too intimidating. The load_instance() function merely takes as its import_resolver parameter anything that can implement the ModuleImportResolver trait. We've already implemented that, so we're in good shape here. Add a few more functions to the file:

wasmi_checkers/src/checkersgame.rs
```
impl CheckersGame {
    pub fn new(module_file: &str) -> CheckersGame {
        let resolver = RuntimeModuleImportResolver::new();

        let instance = load_instance(&resolver, module_file).unwrap();
        let runtime = Runtime::new();

        CheckersGame {
            module_instance: instance,
            runtime,
        }
    }
```
❶
```
    pub fn init(&mut self) -> Result<()> {
        self.module_instance
            .invoke_export("initBoard", &[], &mut self.runtime)?;
        Ok(())
    }
```
❷
```
    pub fn move_piece(&mut self,
                      from: &Coordinate,
                      to: &Coordinate) -> Result<bool> {
        let res = self.module_instance.invoke_export(
            "move",
            &[
                RuntimeValue::from(from.0),
                RuntimeValue::from(from.1),
                RuntimeValue::from(to.0),
                RuntimeValue::from(to.1),
            ],
            &mut self.runtime,
        )?;
```

```
        match res {
            Some(RuntimeValue::I32(v)) => Ok(v != 0),
            _ => {
                println!("Did not get an appropriate response from move.");
                Ok(false)
            }
        }
    }

❸  pub fn get_turn_owner(&mut self) -> Result<PieceColor> {
        let res = self
            .module_instance
            .invoke_export("getTurnOwner", &[], &mut self.runtime)?;
        match res {
            Some(RuntimeValue::I32(v)) => {
                if v == 1 {
                    Ok(PieceColor::Black)
                } else {
                    Ok(PieceColor::White)
                }
            }
            _ => Err(From::from("Bad invocation")),
        }
    }
}
```

❶ A wrapper for the initBoard() module function.

❷ Converts co-ordinate tuples into simple i32s and calls move.

❸ Converts a numeric turn owner from the module to a more API-friendly
enum (PieceColor).

This is great, and so far, we've just been providing idiomatic wrappers around
the WebAssembly module functions. But I think we can do more. For one
thing, we have access to the module's raw linear memory. Since we know how
that module stores the board state, we can grab the raw bytes and convert it
into a way to display the game board.

Since we're writing all the host code in Rust, we have access to some pretty
cool functions, like the ability to do easy-to-read math and read and write
from the module's memory. Take a look at the code we can write to render
the board contents as a string:

wasmi_checkers/src/checkersgame.rs
```
    pub fn get_board_contents(&mut self) -> Result<String> {
        let export = self.module_instance.export_by_name("memory");
        let header = r#"
   0    1   2    3   4    5   6    7
.---.---.---.---.---.---.---.---."#;
        let footer = "    `---^---^---^---^---^---^---^---^";
```

```
        let middle_string = match export {
            Some(ExternVal::Memory(mr)) => gen_board(&mr),
            _ => " -- no board data found -- ".to_string(),
        };

        Ok(format!("{}\n{}{}\n", header, middle_string, footer))
    }
}

fn gen_board(memory: &MemoryRef) -> String {
    let mut vals = Vec::<String>::new();

    for y in 0..8 {
        vals.push(format!("{} ", y));
        for x in 0..8 {
            let offset = calc_offset(x, y);
            let bytevec: Vec<u8> = memory.get(offset, 4).unwrap();
            let value = to_u32(&bytevec[..]);

            vals.push(format!("|{}", value_label(value)));
        }
        vals.push("|\n".into());
    }

    vals.join("")
}

fn value_label(v: u32) -> String {
    match v {
        0 => "   ",
        1 => " B ",
        2 => " W ",
        5 => " B*",
        6 => " W*",
        _ => "???",
    }.into()
}

fn to_u32(bytes: &[u8]) -> u32 {
    bytes.iter().rev().fold(0, |acc, &b| acc * 2 + b as u32)
}

fn calc_offset(x: usize, y: usize) -> u32 {
    ((x + y * 8) * 4) as u32
}
```

The calc_offset() function should look pretty familiar, as we implemented it earlier in the book in the checkers module in wast. Really, the only somewhat complicated piece here is pulling out strips of 4 bytes into a vector and then converting that into a 32-bit unsigned int via the to_u32() function. This version of the function that uses an accumulator and a fold is a little easier to read than some of the "shift left" techniques for coming up with the same result.

Now all we need to do is write our main() function and we should be able to play checkers with a Rust host.

Playing Checkers

Replace whatever your main.rs has with the following code:

```
wasmi_checkers/src/main.rs
extern crate wasmi;

mod checkersgame;
mod imports;
mod runtime;

use checkersgame::CheckersGame;
use std::error::Error;

fn main() -> Result<(), Box<Error>> {
    let mut game = CheckersGame::new("../checkers/checkers.wasm");
    game.init()?;

    let board_display = game.get_board_contents()?;
    println!("game board at start:\n{}\n", board_display);

    println!(
        "At game start, current turn is : {:?}",
        game.get_turn_owner()?
    );
    game.move_piece(&(0, 5), &(0, 4))?;
    println!(
        "After first move, current turn is : {:?}",
        game.get_turn_owner()?
    );

    let board_display = game.get_board_contents()?;
    println!("game board after 1 move:\n{}\n", board_display);

    Ok(())
}
```

The ../checkers/checkers.wasm file here refers to the non-Rust, raw wast version of checkers we built earlier in the book. If you don't want to compile your own, you can grab a copy from the book's resource files.

Let's run it and see what happens:

```
$ cargo run
  Compiling wasmi_checkers v0.1.0
  (file:///home/kevin/Code/Rust/wasmbook/khrust/Book/code/wasmi_checkers)
   Finished dev [unoptimized + debuginfo] target(s) in 0.94s
    Running `target/debug/wasmi_checkers`
```

```
game board at start:
     0   1   2   3   4   5   6   7
   .---.---.---.---.---.---.---.---.
0  |   | W |   | W |   | W |   | W |
1  | W |   | W |   | W |   | W |   |
2  |   | W |   | W |   | W |   | W |
3  |   |   |   |   |   |   |   |   |
4  |   |   |   |   |   |   |   |   |
5  | B |   | B |   | B |   | B |   |
6  |   | B |   | B |   | B |   | B |
7  | B |   | B |   | B |   | B |   |
   `---^---^---^---^---^---^---^---^
```

```
At game start, current turn is : Black
A piece was moved from (0,5) to (0,4)
After first move, current turn is : White
game board after 1 move:
     0   1   2   3   4   5   6   7
   .---.---.---.---.---.---.---.---.
0  |   | W |   | W |   | W |   | W |
1  | W |   | W |   | W |   | W |   |
2  |   | W |   | W |   | W |   | W |
3  |   |   |   |   |   |   |   |   |
4  | B |   |   |   |   |   |   |   |
5  |   |   | B |   | B |   | B |   |
6  |   | B |   | B |   | B |   | B |
7  | B |   | B |   | B |   | B |   |
   `---^---^---^---^---^---^---^---^
```

Not only were we able to flawlessly execute all of the WebAssembly code in the module from a Rust host, but we improved the functionality by wrapping it with our own API and even added an ASCII visualization for the game board.

This same module can now be used interchangeably to play checkers in a web browser, on a console application, or on some kind of server back end, all without making a single change to the compiled wasm file. This is where WebAssembly really shines.

Wrapping Up

You've now taken your WebAssembly skills to the next level. You should now have a deep understanding of how WebAssembly modules interact with their hosts, and what services the hosts provide for those modules. You've seen how web browsers act as hosts and the services they provide, and you've now built a Rust application that can host a WebAssembly module.

Now that you have been able to build this Rust WebAssembly host, it's time to amp up the fun level a little bit. In the next chapter, you will see how WebAssembly's portable binary modules can be used to dramatically improve the development experience with the Internet of Things.

CHAPTER 7

Exploring the Internet of WebAssembly Things

The *Internet of Things (IoT)* is now as ubiquitous as the Internet itself. Some people see this as a tremendous opportunity for growth and innovation while others are terrified of an impending future dominated by millions of woefully underprotected, overconnected devices.

Today we have smart watches, refrigerators, toasters, doorbells, clothing, and thousands of other things that attach the real world to the digital world of the Internet. Infrastucture companies want to sell us platforms to support our IoT applications, security companies want to help us secure our smart devices, and the maker community is constantly expanding and building open source, connected hardware. IoT represents a nearly infinite number of ways to spend and earn money, so it's no wonder it has inspired so much innovation.

As you've come to learn on your journey through this book, WebAssembly is about far more than just speeding up web applications. Its portable, compact format makes it ideal for systems under heavy disk, memory, and processing constraints. It's ideal for isolating business logic from presentation and, as you'll see in this chapter, from external, physical devices.

In this chapter, you'll take advantage of WebAssembly's portability and the Raspberry Pi's easy access to hardware systems to build a pluggable host that separates the logic of determining *what* to display on a hardware indicator from the *how* of displaying it. The LED and computer parts for this chapter's hardware are inexpensive, but even if you don't have a Raspberry Pi, you'll see how you can write and test code for hardware in isolation all from the comfort of your own workstation.

This chapter will operate on, and prove, the following two assumptions:

1. If a WebAssembly module can be hosted in a web browser or a console application, you can host it on a Raspberry Pi

2. If two WebAssembly modules adhere to the same contract, they can be interchanged like modular plugins

Before we start coding, let's take a tour of a use case illustrating the problem we want to solve.

Overview of the Generic Indicator Module

Let's assume that we've been tasked with designing and building part of an IoT project. This project is to build an autonomous wheeled robot that maneuvers its way through an obstacle course as they do in many robotics competitions.

Since we're working as part of a team and there are hundreds of individual pieces on this robot, we've been tasked with handling the *Generic Indicator Module System*. Since all hardware projects need acronyms, we'll call this one *GIMS*. Bonus points for a four-letter acronym, as that puts us just that tiny bit closer to feeling like NASA.

The robot will process multiple streams of sensor inputs from many different devices. GIMS's job is to allow the sensory input to be fed into a WebAssembly module that can then determine how the current state of some aspect of the robot should be visualized. We might have access to gauges, multi-colored LEDs, headlights that could turn on when it's dark—any number of amazing devices.

In some cases, the sensory input might already have been massaged a little bit by the more accurate timing of microcontrollers, while our GIMS will be running on a Raspberry Pi at the very heart of a robot. In this chapter, to keep from writing an entire new book on robotics and WebAssembly, we'll focus solely on the generic indicator system.

The robotics team leadership has built these types of competition robots before, and they know the pain and true price of the integration cost when they have to go back into their code and fuss with tiny details every time they change a piece of hardware. If you haven't played with microcontrollers, "maker kits," or Raspberry Pis, you might assume that LEDs are just LEDs —you control one the same way you control another. The truth is far more annoying.

The reality is that you can go from the simplest LED (apply current, it lights up, *magic!*) to chains of multicolor LEDs that operate with simple timing sequences to systems that use very specific communications protocols like I2C.[1] Changing your peripherals mid-build can be a "stop the world" event, but we can engineer our way around that with a little help from WebAssembly.

With the GIMS design, we'll be putting the indicator logic—which translates a series of sensor inputs into a series of hardware manipulation commands—into WebAssembly. This way, the indicator logic remains isolated and loosely coupled from the physical indicator(s). If someone changes an LED from a simple light-and-resistor to a brick of 200 "LED pixels," they should be able to make a small change to an interface layer and leave our indicator relatively unbothered.

In short, we're taking the software engineering principles of *loose coupling* and *separation of concerns* and, with the power of WebAssembly, bringing them to the world of consumer-grade electronics. The first thing we're going to need to do in order to make that happen is design the contract between the host and the WebAssembly modules.

Designing the Module Contract

As you saw in the chapter on basic JavaScript integration, the contract between a WebAssembly module and its host is a very basic, low-level contract built from numeric primitives. That contract defines how linear memory is accessed, how parameter values can be passed to functions, how we can invoke functions exported from a module, and within the module, invoke functions imported from the host.

Above these low-level bindings, what we need is an API. We need an API that lets the host invoke functions whenever there are new sensor readings available. This API also needs to let the WebAssembly module control the indicator lights. We could even let WebAssembly modules control more hardware like motors and actuators, but that's outside the scope of our GIMS project (though it certainly could be a lot of fun to explore).

First let's think about sensor inputs. I'm sure in real-world circumstances, our sensors would have all different kinds of outputs, and some might have more than one value. But knowing that we're doing this for the Raspberry Pi, and that other microcontrollers closer to the data might be able to massage it for us, it's safe to assume that we'll be able to get a decimal value from each

---

1. i2c.info learn.sparkfun.com/tutorials/i2c

sensor whenever a value changes. So our host is going to want to call a function like the one below to inform our wasm module of a new data point:

```
fn sensor_update(sensor_id: i32, sensor_value: f64) -> f64;
```

Let's say the motor speed is sensor 1, the ambient light detector is sensor 2, the collision detector is sensor 3, the battery of our main laser cannon is 20, etc. We'll have to maintain the Rust-equivalent of a header file so that we can ensure all our modules are operating on the same list of sensors. If the team disagrees on sensor IDs, we're basically back at square 1 and haven't fixed any problems.

Another function we want the host to be able to call is apply(). If we need to animate or update our display over time, we could probably attempt some kind of intricate threading scheme to run each module, but it's far easier to use the "game loop" model and just invoke something like apply() n times per second. We might be able to do fancier things when threading becomes a part of a future version of the WebAssembly specification, but this is good enough for our needs today.

To let the modules know about the passage of time, we can, however, invoke the same function at fixed intervals and pass a *frame* value that increases for each call. We can either agree on a frame rate for updates or write our code so it doesn't really matter:

```
fn apply(frame: i64);
```

For example, an animated indicator might have apply called 20 times per second.

That's it for the input to our modules. Now we need to give the WebAssembly modules a way to control hardware without tightly coupling them to it. For this, we'll abstract over the notion of setting the color of an individual LED with a function that takes an LED index and 3 RGB values between 0 and 255, like so:

```
fn set_led(led_index: i32, r: i32, g: i32, b: i32);
```

If you think back to the fundamentals chapter, recall that while we're allowed to use plenty of data types privately within the module code, we can't import and export higher-level data types like structs. Let's recap and take a look at the three functions in the *GIMS* API contract (import and export are from the point of view of the WebAssembly module) as shown in the table on page 135.

Now that we've got a preliminary contract defined between our hardware host and the wasm modules, we can create a couple of different indicators.

Name	Direction	Params	Returns
apply()	export	• frame	None
sensor_update()	export	• sensor_id • sensor_value	Value
set_led()	import	• led_index • red • green • blue	None

Creating Indicator Modules

Creating an indicator module is really just a matter of creating a regular Rust-based WebAssembly module that adheres to the contract we've defined. You've seen how to create wasm modules using Rust a number of times throughout this book, so it should be easy to get started.

To start, create a root directory that will hold a battery indicator, an animated indicator, and the host application. I chose to call my directory gims, but you can choose whatever you like. As a convenience, to allow you to run builds and tests on all subdirectories at once, you can create a new Cargo.toml in the gims directory with the following contents:

iot_gims/Cargo.toml
```
[workspace]
members = [
  "animatedindicator",
  "batteryindicator",
  "pihost"
]
```

Use cargo new --lib to create the batteryindicator and animatedindicator projects, and cargo new --bin to create the pihost project.

Creating the Battery Indicator

The first indicator module we're going to build is a battery indicator. Its operation is fairly simple: one of the sensor inputs represents the amount of battery remaining as a percentage. In response to that percentage, we're going to control the color of a group of eight LEDs.

These LED indicators are each capable of lighting up with colors comprised of RGB components ranging from 0 through 255. The actual hardware used will be a Blinkt! module from Pimoroni, and I'll include all the details later in case you want to go shopping for your own kits.

Its core logic will be to convert a number from 0-100 into an eight-element array with each element containing an RGB color value—think of it like an LED-based progress bar. For this indicator, we'll divide the percentages among the LEDs and only light them up if the value is >= the base value for that LED. Figuring out the base value for each LED is simple—divide the eight LEDs by 100 and we get 12.5% per LED.

Update your lib.rs with the following code:

iot_gims/batteryindicator/src/lib.rs
```
#[derive(PartialEq, Debug, Clone)]
struct LedColor(i32, i32, i32);

const SENSOR_BATTERY: i32 = 20;

const OFF:LedColor =  LedColor(0, 0, 0);
const YELLOW: LedColor = LedColor(255, 255, 0);
const GREEN: LedColor = LedColor(0, 255, 0);
const RED: LedColor = LedColor(255, 0, 0);
const PCT_PER_PIXEL: f64 = 12.5_f64;

extern "C" {
    fn set_led(led_index: i32, r: i32, g: i32, b: i32);
}

#[no_mangle]
pub extern "C" fn sensor_update(sensor_id: i32, sensor_value: f64) -> f64 {
    if sensor_id == SENSOR_BATTERY {
        set_leds(get_led_values(sensor_value));
    }
    sensor_value
}

#[no_mangle]
pub extern "C" fn apply(_frame: u32) {
    // NO OP, not an animated indicator
}

fn get_led_values(battery_remaining: f64) -> [LedColor; 8] {
    let mut arr: [LedColor; 8] = [OFF,OFF,OFF,OFF,OFF,OFF,OFF,OFF,];
    let lit = (battery_remaining / PCT_PER_PIXEL).ceil();

    // 0 - 20 : Red
    // 21 - <50 : Yellow
    // 51 - 100 : Green

    let color = if 0.0 <= battery_remaining &&
        battery_remaining <= 20.0 {
        RED
```

```
    } else if battery_remaining > 20.0 && battery_remaining < 50.0 {
        YELLOW
    } else {
        GREEN
    };

    for idx in 0..lit as usize {
        arr[idx] = color.clone();
    }

    arr
}
fn set_leds(values: [LedColor; 8]) {
    for x in 0..8 {
        let LedColor(r, g, b) = values[x];
        unsafe {
            set_led(x as i32, r,g,b);
        }
    }
}
```
❺ (marker next to `fn set_leds`)

❶ Create a tuple-struct to hold the three-color codes

❷ Import the set_led() function from our host

❸ Expose the sensor_update() and apply() functions to the host

❹ Core logic to convert a percentage into a set of eight color codes

❺ Invoke the unsafe import in a loop to set all the LED colors on the host

With this code in place, we're going to want to test our module before we plug it into real hardware.

Testing the Battery Indicator

Testing hardware and embedded systems is typically one of the hardest aspects of that kind of development. Pure hardware developers might want to just pull out an oscilloscope and take a look at how the current flows through your system, but this doesn't help us test our business logic (though it could help integration test the host).

Fortunately for us, we don't need to physically test the LEDs right now. We can assume that the host works and write unit tests for our business logic that determines *which* LEDs to light up and what colors to display.

This is where the pluggable modularity of WebAssembly modules starts to truly shine in the embedded and IoT space—finally giving us software developers a way to write unit tests for hardware-bound code without having to rig up elaborate Rube Goldberg machinery to our developer workstations.

This test code (at the bottom of lib.rs) just invokes the get_led_values() function for some known percentages and ensures that we get the right color array in response:

iot_gims/batteryindicator/src/lib.rs
```
#[cfg(test)]
mod tests {

    use {OFF, YELLOW, RED, GREEN, get_led_values};

    #[test]
    fn test_0_pct() {
        assert_eq!(get_led_values(0.0),
            [OFF,OFF,OFF,OFF,OFF,OFF,OFF,OFF,]);
    }

    #[test]
    fn test_15_pct() {
        assert_eq!(get_led_values(15.0),
            [RED, RED, OFF, OFF, OFF, OFF, OFF]);
    }

    #[test]
    fn test_49_pct() {
        assert_eq!(get_led_values(49.0),
            [YELLOW, YELLOW, YELLOW, YELLOW, OFF, OFF, OFF, OFF]);
    }

    #[test]
    fn test_75_pct() {
        assert_eq!(get_led_values(75.0),
            [GREEN,GREEN,GREEN,GREEN,GREEN,GREEN,OFF,OFF,]);
    }

    #[test]
    fn test_100_pct() {
        assert_eq!(get_led_values(100.0),
            [GREEN,GREEN,GREEN,GREEN,GREEN,GREEN,GREEN,GREEN,]);
    }
}
```

You should be able to run cargo test from the root gims directory, and your tests should be invoked, showing output that looks like the following:

```
running 5 tests
test tests::test_0_pct ... ok
test tests::test_100_pct ... ok
test tests::test_49_pct ... ok
test tests::test_15_pct ... ok
test tests::test_75_pct ... ok

test result: ok. 5 passed; 0 failed; 0 ignored; 0 measured; 0 filtered out
```

That's it for the battery indicator, now let's move on to an animated indicator.

Creating the Pulsing Indicator

We have plenty of options available for building an animated indicator. Given that our API is going to be calling apply at a fixed frame rate, it makes sense for us to use a *key frame*[2] animation. Key frame animations are where you define (or interpolate) the values for an animation at given key points or *frames*.

Depending on your age, you might remember the pulsing light built into the front of the K.I.T.T. Pontiac from the old TV series *Knight Rider*. If not, then perhaps the pulsing animated visor in the heads of Cylons from *Battlestar Galactica* is more familiar. Using key frames, this is an incredibly easy animation to create.

Such a "pulser" could represent waiting for a command, an analysis in progress, a pending request to a remote system, or perhaps just to intimidate other robot operators in the competition.

The first thing we want to do is define the key frames. If we think of our eight-light LED strip as an array, then the key frames are actually just the *index* of the currently lit LED. With each successive frame, the "lit index" will move from left to right, take an additional pause on the far right, and then move back to the left again—reproducing the iconic "pulse" animation from *Knight Rider* and/or *Battlestar Galactica*.

You might be shocked by just how little code there is to write:

```
iot_gims/animatedindicator/src/lib.rs
❶ const KEYFRAMES: [i32; 16] = [0,1,2,3,4,5,6,7, 7,6,5,4,3,2,1,0];

❷ extern "C" {
      fn set_led(led_index: i32, r: i32, g: i32, b: i32);
  }

  #[no_mangle]
  pub extern "C" fn sensor_update(_sensor_id: i32, _sensor_value: f64) -> f64 {
      // NO-OP, don't really care about sensor values
      0.0
  }

  #[no_mangle]
  pub extern "C" fn apply(frame: i32) {
      let idx = frame % 16;

❸     for x in 0..8 {
          unsafe {
              set_led(x, 0, 0, 0);
          }
      }
```

---

2.   en.wikipedia.org/wiki/Key_frame

```
    unsafe {
        set_led(KEYFRAMES[idx as usize], 255, 0, 0);
    }
}
```

❶ Define the "lit index" for each of the 16 frames

❷ The exact same imports and exports as the previous module

❸ Ensure that all eight LEDs are dark before we light up the key frame

❹ Call set_led() to turn on the light for the key frame

Since we're guaranteed by the host contract that the frame value will monotonically increase, we just need to grab the modulo 16 of the frame counter to figure out which frame index is lit. We'll also have to assume that the host will reset the frame counter before doing an overflow. Further, the host can change the speed of the pulser by modifying the frequency of apply() calls without us having to modify the WebAssembly module at all.

With our two indicator modules in hand, let's move on to building the Raspberry Pi host.

Building Rust Applications for ARM Devices

Compiling for different target architectures, operating systems, and binary file formats is often an enormous pain in the neck depending on which language and tools you're using. In the past, I've had to set up multiple virtual machines all running concurrently just so I could build the same application for multiple operating systems.

Cargo is an incredibly powerful tool and it comes equipped with the ability to compile for different targets. The rustup command lets you add and remove targets and list all of the available targets. Cross-compilation in Rust is usually quite simple.

Before you can compile for a target other than the default for your operating system, you'll need to install the native compiler for that environment. There's a GitHub repository that's kept up to date with instructions on how to configure your workstation—Linux, Windows, or macOS—for cross-compilation.[3]

The first thing you'll need to do after ensuring your workstation has the native compilation tool chain is to add the appropriate target via rustup. The target for Raspberry Pi 2+ devices is armv7-unknown-linux-gnueabihf. The Raspberry Pi 1 is an ARM v6 device, while all newer ones are ARM v7. The second element

---

3. github.com/japaric/rust-cross

in the target *triple* is the vendor (unknown in our case since it doesn't matter). The third is the operating system and the fourth is the *ABI* (Application Binary Interface). Add the ARM v7 target with the following command:

```
$ rustup target add armv7-unknown-linux-gnueabihf
info: downloading component 'rust-std' for 'armv7-unknown-linux-gnueabihf'
 50.5 MiB /  50.5 MiB (100 %)   6.5 MiB/s ETA:   0 s
info: installing component 'rust-std' for 'armv7-unknown-linux-gnueabihf'
```

Next, configure Cargo for cross-compilation using the instructions on the GitHub repository. For Ubuntu Linux, it will look like this:

```
$ mkdir -p ~/.cargo
$ cat >>~/.cargo/config <<EOF
> [target.armv7-unknown-linux-gnueabihf]
> linker = "arm-linux-gnueabihf-gcc"
> EOF
```

Next, create a new Rust binary application using the same commands you've been using throughout the book. To compile this application so it will run on a Raspberry Pi, use the following command (which looks very similar to how we specify the WebAssembly target for wasm compilation):

```
$ cargo build --target armv7-unknown-linux-gnueabihf
Compiling crosscompiledemo v0.1.0
  (file:///home/kevin/Code/Rust/wasmbook/khrust/Book/code/crosscompiledemo)
Finished dev [unoptimized + debuginfo] target(s) in 0.58s
```

Finally, to verify that this new binary is actually an ARM v7 Linux binary and not a binary for the development workstation that ran the build, you can execute the following command:

```
$ file target/armv7-unknown-linux-gnueabihf/debug/crosscompiledemo
target/armv7-unknown-linux-gnueabihf/debug/crosscompiledemo:
ELF 32-bit LSB shared object, ARM, EABI5 version 1 (SYSV),
dynamically linked, interpreter /lib/ld-linux-armhf.so.3,
for GNU/Linux 3.2.0, BuildID[sha1]=fb1690370f7516f436c440d5083447d8fe06077a,
with debug_info, not stripped
```

If you've got a Raspberry Pi (2 or newer) handy, you can take the single cross-compiledemo binary and scp that to the device and execute it. You should see the standard "Hello, World" text. Now that your workstation is set up to do cross-compilation for ARM v7, it's time to build the indicator module host.

Hosting Indicator Modules on a Raspberry Pi

To build an application that resides on a Raspberry Pi (but that we can test on our workstations) that hosts our indicator modules, we'll need to employ a few techniques that we haven't covered in this book yet. The requirements for our *Generic Indicator Module System* are as follows:

- Load a WebAssembly module at launch and immediately run, controlling LEDs

- Enforce a fixed frame rate for animated modules

- Trap the *SIGINT* and *SIGTERM* signals, gracefully turning off active LEDs before shutdown

- *Hot Reloading*—if a new module is copied into a monitored location, pause, then load the new module and continue

The application is designed to start and continue running forever, constantly getting new sensor inputs (though we're only faking one sensor) and feeding that data to the indicator module. To make all of this work, you'll get into some new Rust patterns like using multi-threaded code, channels, and conditional compilation.

Creating a Raspberry Pi Application

In the previous section, you created an empty application called pihost. At the moment there's nothing special that you need to do to make this application suitable for a Raspberry Pi. We do need to pick some dependencies—crates that will help us monitor the file system, read and execute WebAssembly modules, respond to OS signals, and operate the *Blinkt* hardware module. This is a Cargo.toml that pulls in those dependencies:

```
iot_gims/pihost/Cargo.toml
[package]
name = "pihost"
version = "0.1.0"
authors = ["your Email <your@email.com>"]

[dependencies]
notify = "4.0.0"
wasmi = "0.4.1"
ctrlc = { version = "3.0", features = ["termination"] }

[target.'cfg(any(target_arch = "arm", target_arch = "armv7"))'.dependencies]
blinkt = "0.4.0"
```

This is the first time you've seen *conditional compilation* in action. The highlighted lines will only include the blinkt dependency when you're compiling for the *ARM* architecture.

Watching for New Modules

There are a number of mission-critical tasks in the application and, as you'll see, coordinating them can be really tricky. Thankfully Rust makes it pretty easy. The first task is monitoring the file system and then letting the main module runner know that it needs to reload a module. The following two functions make that possible:

```
iot_gims/pihost/src/main.rs
#[cfg(any(target_arch = "armv7", target_arch = "arm"))]
extern crate blinkt;

extern crate ctrlc;
extern crate notify;
extern crate wasmi;

use notify::{DebouncedEvent, RecommendedWatcher, RecursiveMode, Watcher};
use std::path::Path;
use std::sync::mpsc::{channel, RecvTimeoutError, Sender};
use std::thread;
use std::time::Duration;
use wasm::Runtime;
use wasmi::RuntimeValue;

const MODULE_FILE: &'static str = "/home/kevin/indicators/indicator.wasm";
const MODULE_DIR: &'static str = "/home/kevin/indicators";

enum RunnerCommand {
    Reload,
    Stop,
}

fn watch(tx_wasm: Sender<RunnerCommand>) -> notify::Result<()> {
    let (tx, rx) = channel();

    let mut watcher: RecommendedWatcher =
        Watcher::new(tx, Duration::from_secs(1))?;
    watcher.watch(MODULE_DIR, RecursiveMode::NonRecursive)?;

    loop {
        match rx.recv() {
            Ok(event) => handle_event(event, &tx_wasm),
            Err(e) => println!("watch error: {:?}", e),
        }
    }
}

fn handle_event(event: DebouncedEvent, tx_wasm: &Sender<RunnerCommand>) {
    match event {
        DebouncedEvent::NoticeWrite(path) => {
            let path = Path::new(&path);
            let filename = path.file_name().unwrap();
            if filename == "indicator.wasm" {
                tx_wasm.send(RunnerCommand::Reload).unwrap();
```

```
            } else {
                println!("write (unexpected file): {:?}", path);
            }
        }
        _ => {}
    }
}
```

❶ Creates a *multi-producer, single-consumer* communication channel

❷ Block the receive channel until a message arrives

❸ Send a message on the channel, indicating that we should reload the WebAssembly module

In Rust, multi-producer-single-consumer (*mpsc*) channels are used as a safe way to communicate between threads. In the case of the watch() function, the main thread sits in a loop, awaiting file system notifications from the monitored directory. When we see the NoticeWrite event, it's time to tell another thread to reload the module from disk.

Creating the Module Runner Thread

In the last section, you saw code that sends a message on a channel to tell another thread to reload a WebAssembly module. In this section, you'll create that main thread. This thread has a number of jobs. It obviously needs to listen for the RunnerCommand::Reload message, but it also needs to handle the RunnerCommand::Stop message (which it will get from us monitoring OS signals). It also needs to invoke methods on the module itself, setting the fake sensor input value and calling apply() to take care of animations.

This is where it would be *so* much easier to throw up our hands and walk away. Juggling file system monitoring, two different threads, signal trapping, *and* ensuring a consistent frame rate in the WebAssembly module sounds as complicated as dealing with the three-body problem.[4]

Luckily, there's a solution that doesn't require creating yet another coordination thread. Instead, we can use the *timeout* feature of channel receives. If we wait for the inverse of the frame rate in milliseconds for a message to arrive, and no messages comes, then we can invoke the apply() function on the WebAssembly module. For example, if we want to enforce 20fps, then we would set our receive timeout delay to 50 milliseconds. For a frame rate of 10fps, we'd set the delay to 100 milliseconds, which actually produces a pretty good effect on the Blinkt hardware.

---

4. en.wikipedia.org/wiki/Three-body_problem

Let's take a look at the code for the main() function (anything from the wasm module is code that we'll write shortly):

```
iot_gims/pihost/src/main.rs
fn main() {
    let (tx_wasm, rx_wasm) = channel();
    let _indicator_runner = thread::spawn(move || {
        let mut runtime = Runtime::new();
        let mut module = wasm::get_module_instance(MODULE_FILE);
        println!("Starting wasm runner thread...");
        loop {
❶           match rx_wasm.recv_timeout(Duration::from_millis(100)) {
                Ok(RunnerCommand::Reload) => {
                    println!("Received a reload signal, sleeping for 2s");
                    thread::sleep(Duration::from_secs(2));
                    module = wasm::get_module_instance(MODULE_FILE);
                }
                Ok(RunnerCommand::Stop) => {
                    runtime.shutdown();
                    break;
                }
                Err(RecvTimeoutError::Timeout) => {
                    runtime.reduce_battery();
                    runtime.advance_frame();
                    module
                        .invoke_export(
                            "sensor_update",
                            &[
                                RuntimeValue::from(wasm::SENSOR_BATTERY),
                                RuntimeValue::F64(
                                  runtime.remaining_battery.into()),
                            ][..],
                            &mut runtime,
                        ).unwrap();

                    module
                        .invoke_export(
                            "apply",
                            &[RuntimeValue::from(runtime.frame)][..],
                            &mut runtime,
                        ).unwrap();
                }
                Err(_) => break,
            }
        }
    });

❷   let tx_wasm_sig = tx_wasm.clone();

❸   ctrlc::set_handler(move || {
        tx_wasm_sig.send(RunnerCommand::Stop).unwrap();
    }).expect("Error setting Ctrl-C handler");
```

```
❹      if let Err(e) = watch(tx_wasm) {
           println!("error: {:?}", e)
       }
}

mod wasm;
```

❶ Enforce the frame rate with a 100ms timeout value on receive

❷ Send channels can be cloned, hence their presence in the multi-producer module

❸ Use the ctrlc crate to trap SIGTERM and SIGINT, sending a Stop command in response

❹ The watch() function blocks the main thread with an infinite loop

Creating the WebAssembly Module Runtime

Let's create the wasm.rs module that was referenced by the previous set of code:

iot_gims/pihost/src/wasm.rs
```
use std::fmt;
use std::fs::File;
use wasmi::{
    Error as InterpreterError, Externals, FuncInstance, FuncRef,
    HostError, ImportsBuilder, Module, ModuleImportResolver, ModuleInstance,
    ModuleRef, RuntimeArgs, RuntimeValue, Signature, Trap, ValueType,
};
```
❶
```
#[cfg(any(target_arch = "armv7", target_arch = "arm"))]
use blinkt::Blinkt;

fn load_module(path: &str) -> Module {
    use std::io::prelude::*;
    let mut file = File::open(path).unwrap();
    let mut wasm_buf = Vec::new();
    file.read_to_end(&mut wasm_buf).unwrap();
    Module::from_buffer(&wasm_buf).unwrap()
}

pub fn get_module_instance(path: &str) -> ModuleRef {
    let module = load_module(path);
    let mut imports = ImportsBuilder::new();
    imports.push_resolver("env", &RuntimeModuleImportResolver);

    ModuleInstance::new(&module, &imports)
        .expect("Failed to instantiate module")
        .assert_no_start()
}
pub const SENSOR_BATTERY: i32 = 20;
```

```rust
#[derive(Debug)]
pub enum Error {
    Interpreter(InterpreterError),
}

impl fmt::Display for Error {
    fn fmt(&self, f: &mut fmt::Formatter) -> fmt::Result {
        write!(f, "{:?}", self)
    }
}

impl From<InterpreterError> for Error {
    fn from(e: InterpreterError) -> Self {
        Error::Interpreter(e)
    }
}

impl HostError for Error {}

pub struct Runtime {
    #[cfg(any(target_arch = "armv7", target_arch = "arm"))]
    blinkt: Blinkt,
    pub frame: i32,
    pub remaining_battery: f64,
}

impl Runtime {
    #[cfg(any(target_arch = "armv7", target_arch = "arm"))]
    pub fn new() -> Runtime {
        println!("Instiantiating WASM runtime (ARM)");
        Runtime {
            blinkt: Blinkt::new().unwrap(),
            frame: 0,
            remaining_battery: 100.0,
        }
    }

    #[cfg(not(any(target_arch = "armv7", target_arch = "arm")))]
    pub fn new() -> Runtime {
        println!("Instantiating WASM runtime (non-ARM)");
        Runtime {
            frame: 0,
            remaining_battery: 100.0,
        }
    }
}

impl Externals for Runtime {
    fn invoke_index(
        &mut self,
        index: usize,
        args: RuntimeArgs,
    ) -> Result<Option<RuntimeValue>, Trap> {
```

```
        match index {
            0 => {
                let idx: i32 = args.nth(0);
                let red: i32 = args.nth(1);
                let green: i32 = args.nth(2);
                let blue: i32 = args.nth(3);
                self.set_led(idx, red, green, blue);
                Ok(None)
            }
            _ => panic!("Unknown function index!"),
        }
    }
}

impl Runtime {
    #[cfg(not(any(target_arch = "armv7", target_arch = "arm")))]
    fn set_led(&self, idx: i32, red: i32, green: i32, blue: i32) {
        println!("[LED {}]: {}, {}, {}", idx, red, green, blue);
    }

    #[cfg(any(target_arch = "armv7", target_arch = "arm"))]
    fn set_led(&mut self, idx: i32, red: i32, green: i32, blue: i32) {
        self.blinkt
            .set_pixel(idx as usize, red as u8, green as u8, blue as u8);
        self.blinkt.show().unwrap();
    }

    #[cfg(not(any(target_arch = "armv7", target_arch = "arm")))]
    pub fn shutdown(&mut self) {
        println!("WASM runtime shut down.");
        self.halt();
    }

    #[cfg(any(target_arch = "armv7", target_arch = "arm"))]
    pub fn shutdown(&mut self) {
        println!("WASM runtime shut down.");
        self.blinkt.clear();
        self.blinkt.cleanup().unwrap();
        self.halt();
    }

    fn halt(&self) {
        ::std::process::exit(0);
    }

    pub fn reduce_battery(&mut self) {
        self.remaining_battery -= 1.0;
        if self.remaining_battery < 0.0 {
            self.remaining_battery = 100.0;
        }
    }

    pub fn advance_frame(&mut self) {
        self.frame += 1;
```

```
        if self.frame > 1_000_000_000 {
            self.frame = 0;
        }
    }
}

struct RuntimeModuleImportResolver;

impl<'a> ModuleImportResolver for RuntimeModuleImportResolver {
    fn resolve_func(
        &self,
        field_name: &str,
        _signature: &Signature,
    ) -> Result<FuncRef, InterpreterError> {
        println!("Resolving {}", field_name);
        let func_ref = match field_name {
            "set_led" => FuncInstance::alloc_host(
                Signature::new(
                    &[
                        ValueType::I32,
                        ValueType::I32,
                        ValueType::I32,
                        ValueType::I32,
                    ][..],
                    None,
                ),
                0,
            ),
            _ => {
                return Err(InterpreterError::Function(format!(
                    "host module doesn't export function with name {}",
                    field_name
                )))
            }
        };
        Ok(func_ref)
    }
}
```

❶ Conditionally add Blinkt to the module's scope

❷ Conditionally add a blinkt field to the Runtime struct

❸ The apply() function will have an index of 0.

❹ The set_led() function is the only one exported by the host/imported by the module

Most of this should look pretty familiar to you as a lot of it is just the boiler-plate required to load the WebAssembly module, resolve its imports, and allow function calls.

You may have noticed one interesting thing: because of the conditional compilation, there are actually multiple functions with the same name. If we are building for ARM, then the Runtime struct gets an extra field called blinkt and the set_led() function uses that field to control real hardware, whereas the "regular" version of that struct and function just emit debug text to the console.

Running the Application

To run the application on your workstation, just build the binary and execute it or type cargo run. This will launch the application and it will load the module at /home/kevin/indicators/indicator.wasm (feel free to change that location to suit your needs).

Running on a Mac, Windows, or Linux, you'll see some console output spam as the module tells the host what LEDs to light up 10 times per second (the following is output from the animated pulse indicator):

```
Instantiating Wasm runtime (non-ARM)
Resolving set_led
Starting wasm runner thread...
[LED 0]: 0, 0, 0
[LED 1]: 0, 0, 0
[LED 2]: 0, 0, 0
[LED 3]: 0, 0, 0
[LED 4]: 0, 0, 0
[LED 5]: 0, 0, 0
[LED 6]: 0, 0, 0
[LED 7]: 0, 0, 0
[LED 1]: 255, 0, 0
[LED 0]: 0, 0, 0
[LED 1]: 0, 0, 0
[LED 2]: 0, 0, 0
[LED 3]: 0, 0, 0
[LED 4]: 0, 0, 0
[LED 5]: 0, 0, 0
[LED 6]: 0, 0, 0
^CWasm runtime shut down.
```

Here I've tested the signal handling capabilities and the application shut down nicely in response to a Control-C. Next, we can try this out on real hardware.

Hardware Shopping List

Before you can run this code on a Raspberry Pi host, you're obviously going to need a Raspberry Pi. For my own testing I used a Raspberry Pi 3 and I communicated with it via ssh over WiFi. You should be able to use a Raspberry

Pi 2 as well. These devices are pretty inexpensive to obtain in the US, though price and availability does tend to fluctuate globally. If you can't buy one, see if you can find a local *makers* group. They tend to have plenty of spares for testing and experimentation.

Next, you'll need a Pimoroni Blinkt.[5] These are amazing little devices and, at the time I write this, only cost $6. They come with pins and fit snugly right onto the GPIO ports of your Raspberry Pi.

For my own version, I bought a *Mini Black Hat Hack3r*,[6] which allows you to attach a ribbon cable to your Pi's GPIO ports and extend them outside its case. It's like a GPIO "extension cord." You'll see the one I used in the demonstration video. I like the flexibility of this as it lets me keep some of my custom Raspberry Pi cases, but you certainly don't need one to run the application.

That's it—that's all you need to run this demo, assuming your Pi has network access and a power supply. Don't power it from a computer's USB, power it from the wall. I've seen the drain from similar LEDs cause the power to "flicker" on the Pi causing it to reboot.

Running the Application on a Raspberry Pi

Now that you've got your hardware all set and your Blinkt is plugged into your Raspberry Pi, it's time to play with some lights. First, scp the pihost binary to somewhere on the Pi. I just used the pi user's home directory. Your Raspberry Pi OS and configuration may vary depending on whether you installed *Raspbian*[7] or another distribution. Check your distribution's documentation if you have trouble logging into the default user and creating directories.

Next, scp the batteryindicator.wasm and animatedindicator.wasm files onto the Pi. I also put these in the pi user's home directory, but you can put them anywhere.

You'll need to create and set the permissions on the indicator modules directory. The chapter code has this set for /home/kevin/indicators, but you can change that to whatever you like and recompile. You might need to sudo the commands to create those directories.

Finally, make sure the application can read from the indicator directory and that you won't have any problems writing to it:

```
$ chmod -R a+rw /home/kevin/indicators
```

---

5. shop.pimoroni.com/products/blinkt
6. www.adafruit.com/product/3182
7. www.raspberrypi.org/downloads/raspbian/

This grants global read/write access to that directory. In a production system, you'd probably want to be more careful about your permissions, but it's fine for testing.

Copy one of the indicator wasm files to the indicator directory and make sure to call it indicator.wasm. While ssh'd into the Raspberry Pi, start the pihost executable. You should see the Blinkt immediately light up (it's *super bright*) and start going through the pattern of whatever indicator you chose. The battery indicator will slowly make its way to "off" and then start over, while the animated indicator will show a single red LED pulsing back and forth.

Now for the really fun part—with the application still running, copy a different indicator onto the indicator.wasm file. You'll see the lights pause for a few seconds, then it'll switch to the new indicator pattern and continue on its merry way, as you'll see in this YouTube video.[8]

Endless Possibilities

I've asked you a couple times in this book to pause and reflect on your accomplishments and what you've been able to do with WebAssembly. Now let's reflect on those reflections, but with the added perspective of knowing that we can build portable, immutable binaries that can snap into applications running attached to hardware, running on our laptops, running on servers, or running in browsers.

Thinking about this fires just about every neuron in my brain. Just think, you could create autopilot software for drones in WebAssembly and swap out different "brains" without ever needing to do anything to the drone itself. You could test this software in 3D rendered desktop environments or in browsers, all without ever having to modify the WebAssembly module. These drone hosts could go from a search-and-rescue mission to playing Quidditch[9] with nothing more than an an over-the-air software update.

Factories, manufacturing facilities, power plants, and building management systems, all of which are normally tightly coupled to their hardware, could all benefit from this. Many of these places operate with hundreds of *PLCs* (Programmable Logic Controller) that interface with, monitor, and control all kinds of machines as shown in the figure on page 153.

What if instead of using languages like ladder diagrams or function blocks to program PLCs, we could just drop WebAssembly modules into them that

---

8.   www.youtube.com/watch?v=bZAyOD_vSVg
9.   en.wikipedia.org/wiki/Quidditch

adhered to a well-known specification? Then we could use whatever language we wanted to produce testable, verifiable, portable logic controllers that could control anything a PLC can control today.

WebAssembly files are just binary files. That means that we can encrypt them and we can digitally sign them. There are a ton of things that you could do to add a layer of security to using WebAssembly modules that might one day be able to prevent things like PLC viruses.[10]

With all of this talk of hardware, I have not forgotten the idea of using WebAssembly to build in-browser applications—far from it. You could spend all of your WebAssembly time doing nothing but building browser applications and never run out of things to do or build. But there's a bigger picture here. WebAssembly is bigger than the web, it's bigger than just IoT, and it's bigger than most people give it credit for. Hopefully this little section of the book has inspired you, and you're cooking up the next amazing thing right now—all based on WebAssembly.

---

10. en.wikipedia.org/wiki/Stuxnet

Wrapping Up

In this chapter, we illustrated a number of really powerful techniques and we got into some more detail with the Rust programming language. You saw how to set up your workstation to cross-compile Rust applications for multiple platforms, including the Raspberry Pi. You read about how to conditionally compile different pieces of your codebase depending on your target architecture, and you saw how to coordinate multiple parallel activities in Rust with threads and channels.

You also got to see Rust playing host to WebAssembly modules and providing a bridge to controllable hardware like LED blocks to give WebAssembly incredible abilities. We built an application that can hot-swap LED controller modules without even needing a restart.

As you'll see in the next chapter, we can take our knowledge of hosting WebAssembly outside the browser straight to the cloud, and leverage new technologies like *FaaS* (Functions as a Service) and serverless to deploy WebAssembly modules in our back end as well as in the browser.

CHAPTER 8

Building WARoS—
The WebAssembly Robot System

We started this book by going over the fundamentals of what WebAssembly is, how it works, and what its raw text format looks like. In later chapters, you learned how to build WebAssembly modules that can interact with browser hosts and use advanced UI libraries to build full-featured "pure WebAssembly" web applications.

Then we ventured into the realm of non-browser hosts, and you learned how to write Rust code that can load, validate, and interpret a WebAssembly module. We put this into action by writing a console-based checkers host and even a Raspberry Pi host that allowed a WebAssembly module to manipulate LEDs.

In this chapter, you're going to take everything you've learned and apply it to building a Rust host that can load multiple WebAssembly "robots" into a virtual arena, pit them against each other, and run all of the game logic. You'll not only learn how to build this code, but I'll also illustrate multiple extension points where you can add a ton of cool, cloud-based features to this game.

This chapter will be the heaviest in terms of exposure to advanced Rust topics, like shared, mutable state across threads and some pretty intricate use of *borrows* and *moves*. While building the game in this chapter, you'll learn a lot about Rust, and the game will provide a fun tool you can use to continue learning and exploring Rust and WebAssembly.

An Homage to Crobots

Back in December of 1985, Tom Poindexter released a game called *Crobots*.[1] This game combined a custom C compiler and a stack-based virtual machine that compiled robot files written in a C-like subset and evaluated combat between multiple robots. This program compiled multiple robots, and then it could either display live results or just give you a summary of the match when it was over. Crobots was ahead of its time and, despite the relative lack of raw computing power of the era, it was, for all intents and purposes, *real-time* (limited by hardware clock speeds and a couple of other factors).

It wasn't just a game, however. Crobots' simplified C syntax and narrowly focused goal (kill your opponents without dying) made it an amazing tool to introduce programming languages and computer science concepts to eager learners. When I was 11 years old, I asked my grandfather if he could teach me C, as I'd just finished learning BASIC. He handed me the Crobots floppy disk and a printed copy of the documentation (complete with dot matrix feeder holes!) and left me to my own devices.

I taught myself C and a number of vital programming concepts by learning to build robots to compete against others. I was instantly entranced by the concepts of virtual worlds, computer programming, and game design theory. The rest, as they say, is history. I quite literally owe much of what I've been able to accomplish in my career to my childhood exposure to Tom Poindexter's creation, and of course, to my grandfather for giving it to me.

The Rules of Crobots

The documentation for the original Crobots game is now available online.[2] You don't need to read the original in order to implement the WebAssembly game, but I thoroughly enjoyed reading it for the pure nostalgia value.

Each robot in the game is essentially a tank. It can move in any direction by engaging its drive motor pointing in a direction indicated by a *heading* angle between 0 and 360 degrees. It also has an independently mounted cannon that can fire in any direction indicated by the same type of heading. Each robot's compass is calibrated with East pointing to the right, as shown in the figure on page 157.

All of the robots occupy a 1,000m by 1,000m battlefield. The perimeter wall is dangerous and inflicts damage to robots upon collision. Robots colliding

---

1. en.wikipedia.org/wiki/Crobots
2. crobots.deepthought.it/html/manual.html#5.

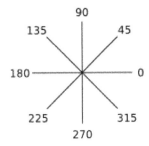

with each other also take damage. If you want your robot to survive and kill all of your opponents, your robot is going to need *input*.

The most important input is the *scanner*. All robot scanners have a range of 700m and can scan within an arc your robot specifies, with a maximum spread of 10 degrees. Damage in the game is doled out according to the following table:

Damage	Description
2%	Robot vs. robot or robot vs. wall collision. Also stops the drive motor, setting the speed to 0.
3%	Missile explodes within a 40m radius of robot
5%	Missile explodes within a 20m radius
10%	Missile explodes within a 10m radius

Other inputs include status information, such as the robot's current location. There are some subtleties missing from the robot API, and so you'll need to keep track of some information yourself like your current destination, your last heading, and so on. One final rule is that while every robot has an unlimited supply of missiles, only two missiles can ever be in the air at a given time.

Now that we've got the basic rules defined, let's try and build an API that gives robots the tools they need for real-time combat.

Designing the WARoS API

The original Crobots API was defined by what Poindexter called the *Intrinsic Function Library*.[3] Each of these functions were made available to the original robots to allow them to interact with (and hopefully dominate) their virtual environment. If you're thinking that this sounds a lot like a list of imports required by a WebAssembly module, you're right. As soon as I remembered the Crobots intrinsic functions, I *knew* I had to try and port it to WebAssembly.

---

3. crobots.deepthought.it/html/manual.html#8

Let's take a look at the original list of intrinsic functions:

Function	Description
scan(deg, res)	Invokes the robot's scanner, pointing it at a specified degree and resolution. Returns 0 if there are no robots in range. Otherwise returns a positive integer indicating the distance to the closest target in that direction.
cannon(deg, range)	Fires the cannon at a specified degree and range. Range is limited to 700m. Returns 0 if no missile was fired, 1 if a missile was fired.
drive(deg, speed)	Engages the drive motor in the specified direction at the indicated percentage of power.
damage()	Returns the percentage of damage currently taken by the robot.
speed()	Returns the current speed of the robot as a percent. Check this value as it can differ from the parameter given to drive because of acceleration, deceleration, and collisions
loc_x() loc_y()	Returns the current x- or y-coordinate.
rand(limit)	Returns a random number between 0 and limit, with a max of 32,767
sqrt(number)	Returns the square root of a number, coerced positive if necessary
sin(deg) cos(deg) tan(deg) atan(deg)	Trig functions. In the original Crobots game, in-memory trig tables and a large scale were used to avoid floating-point calculations and roundoff problems. We shouldn't need to use any of those tricks with our API.

Converting the Crobots Intrinsic Functions into a Rust API

When I first went back and looked at the Crobots documentation, I was struck by the elegance of the intrinsic function library. If you take a close look, you'll see that all of the functions already adhere to the basic rules that we know apply to WebAssembly modules—nothing takes or returns any parameter that isn't a 32-bit integer, and there are no complex types or tuples used.

WebAssembly has floating-point numbers, but this list of functions has been working quite well for decades, so let's stick with it and see how well it works out for a modern game. The first step is converting these functions into a list of extern functions.

To start off, let's create a workspace in a root directory (I called mine waros) and then create a new Rust library project beneath that called warsdk. This will be a library used to wrap extern functions and provide a few other utilities to WebAssembly robot modules.

Ignore the lib.rs for now and create a new file called ffi.rs. FFI stands for *Foreign Function Interface*, and the extern declarations are part of Rust's FFI:

```
waros/warsdk/src/ffi.rs
extern "C" {
    pub fn scan(angle: i32, resolution: i32) -> i32;
    pub fn cannon(angle: i32, range: i32) -> i32;
    pub fn drive(angle: i32, speed: i32) -> i32;
    pub fn damage() -> i32;
    pub fn speed() -> i32;
    pub fn loc_x() -> i32;
    pub fn loc_y() -> i32;
    pub fn rand(limit: i32) -> i32;
    pub fn wsqrt(number: i32) -> i32;
    pub fn wsin(degree: i32) -> i32;
    pub fn wcos(degree: i32) -> i32;
    pub fn wtan(degree: i32) -> i32;
    pub fn watan(degree: i32) -> i32;
    pub fn plot_course(tx: i32, ty: i32) -> i32;
}
```

Most of this looks identical to Poindexter's original intrinsic function list, with a few minor changes. First, I had to add a prefix to a few of the math functions because, after a recent Rust update, functions like sin and cos were made part of a globally visible set of names and wouldn't link to WebAssembly anymore.

Second, I added a function called plot_course(). This just determines the heading from the robot's current location to a target location. Nearly every Robot that chooses a destination coordinate will need this function, so I made it part of the API for convenience.

Keeping It Simple

While building this sample, I tried computing the heading inside one of the robot's code. Interestingly, this compiled Wasm module demanded that the host support a function called Math_atan2(). I'd used atan2() in an early version of the code, and instead of preventing my compilation, the compiler decided it should make the host provide that function. As you start adding complexity to your robot modules, you might see something like this happen again.

This looks like a pretty simple API, and it should be easy for developers working in Rust, Go, raw WebAssembly, or any other language to build robots compatible with the host. People building robots in lower-level languages will be thankful for the availability of the trig functions and it also helps us ensure that robots from different languages behave consistently within the same host.

I placed these extern functions in their own FFI module so that the name exposed to the SDK consumers (the robot developers) could have the same names and still wrap the external calls in unsafe. Modify the lib.rs file of the warsdk project to look like this:

waros/warsdk/src/lib.rs
```rust
pub fn scan(angle: i32, resolution: i32) -> i32 {
    unsafe { ffi::scan(angle, resolution) }
}

pub fn cannon(angle: i32, range: i32) -> i32 {
    unsafe { ffi::cannon(angle, range) }
}

pub fn drive(angle: i32, speed: i32) -> i32 {
    unsafe { ffi::drive(angle, speed) }
}

pub fn damage() -> i32 {
    unsafe { ffi::damage() }
}

pub fn speed() -> i32 {
    unsafe { ffi::speed() }
}

pub fn loc_x() -> i32 {
    unsafe { ffi::loc_x() }
}

pub fn loc_y() -> i32 {
    unsafe { ffi::loc_y() }
}

pub fn rand(limit: i32) -> i32 {
    unsafe { ffi::rand(limit) }
}

pub fn wsqrt(number: i32) -> i32 {
    unsafe { ffi::wsqrt(number) }
}

pub fn wsin(degree: i32) -> i32 {
    unsafe { ffi::wsin(degree) }
}
pub fn wcos(degree: i32) -> i32 {
    unsafe { ffi::wcos(degree) }
}
```

```rust
pub fn wtan(degree: i32) -> i32 {
    unsafe { ffi::wtan(degree) }
}

pub fn watan(degree: i32) -> i32 {
    unsafe { ffi::watan(degree) }
}

pub fn plot_course(tx: i32, ty: i32) -> i32 {
    unsafe { ffi::plot_course(tx, ty) }
}

// Utility sample for moving to destination and stopping
// Note - does NOT recover from collision en route
pub fn go(target_x: i32, target_y: i32) {
    let course = plot_course(target_x, target_y);
    drive(course, 20);
    // at speed 20, it should take 2 ticks from awareness
    // of the target to stop on it
    while (target_x - loc_x()).abs() > 40 &&
          (target_y - loc_y()).abs() > 40 &&
            speed() > 0 {
        // wait till we get to the target
    }

    drive(course, 0); // turn off engine
    while speed() > 0 {
        // steady on until we stop
    }
}

pub const ANGLE_EAST: i32 = 0;
pub const ANGLE_NORTH: i32 = 90;
pub const ANGLE_WEST: i32 = 180;
pub const ANGLE_SOUTH: i32 = 270;

pub const MAX_X: u32 = 1000;
pub const MAX_Y: u32 = 1000;

pub const DAMAGE_COLLISION: u32 = 2;
pub const DAMAGE_DIRECTHIT: u32 = 10;
pub const DAMAGE_NEARHIT: u32 = 5;
pub const DAMAGE_FAR_HIT: u32 = 3;

pub const BLAST_RADIUS: i32 = 40;

pub const PROJECTILE_MAX_RANGE: u32 = 200;

mod ffi;
```

Most of this is just simple unsafe wrappers around the extern functions. However, I've added a handy little utility function called go() that was useful enough to include in the SDK rather than individual robots. There are also a couple of constants available to help robot developers write logic. Be warned, though—these aren't the constants built into the game engine itself, so there's a risk of getting them out of sync. This might be an issue if you were publishing this SDK outside of book samples. Each time you want to build a robot in WebAssembly and Rust, you'll just declare a dependency on this SDK.

Finally, the Cargo.toml can stay the way it came out of the initial creation. Add a line to your workspace's root Cargo.toml so it looks like this:

```
[workspace]
members = [
  "warsdk",
]
```

Now everything we're going to build in this chapter (and there will be a lot) will build to the root-level target directory and you can run test suites at the top level for all of your projects.

Building the WARoS Match Engine

The WARoS *match engine* will be responsible for the following:

- Provide a host runtime for each WebAssembly module
- Provide a *game loop* for moving the match forward
- Manage game state
- Complete a match after a given number of cycles

Building a game engine is no small feat. The goal of what we're building in this chapter isn't to produce the best game engine. It's to illustrate how we can host multiple WebAssembly modules simultaneously within a virtual environment and allow their logic to safely interact and manipulate shared state. In the following sections, you'll see how to accomplish all of this with Rust.

Threading, Time Slicing, and the Game Loop

Building games and game engines is loads of fun for certain types of people, like myself, who have often been referred to as masochists due to the depth and complexity of some of the problems that need to be solved in this domain. One of the problems we encounter when building game engines, *the game loop*, also shows up in a surprising number of other types of software, including big enterprise apps.

In Poindexter's original implementation, he created his own virtual CPU. This meant that for each robot loaded into memory, he could control the allocation of time. Specifically, he could dole out processing cycles to each robot in turn. This allowed the robot code to be written in a way that *felt* real-time. The robots all operate within while loops that control their behavior throughout the match.

With WebAssembly, we don't have that luxury. We aren't in control of the time-slicing mechanism *inside* the module, and the WebAssembly standard doesn't even have any formal definition for internal threading or atomic locking (at the time this book was written). I really wanted to maintain the "robot loop" feel of the original robot code, and so this presented a huge problem—how do I let each WebAssembly module run its own tight, infinite loop without blocking everything, gumming up the works, or worse, running afoul of Rust's ever-vigilant borrow checker?

As I looked for solutions, I discovered that this type of problem of time sharing among multiple threads shows up in a lot of places. If you spend most of your time working in high-level web or data access frameworks, you're probably insulated from the solutions to this concurrency problem, but they're there if you want to look.

My initial solution was to spin up a single Rust thread for each WebAssembly module, in which the module would be allowed to run its infinite loop (triggered by the bot_init() exported function). Then, I'd run a traditional *game loop*[4] that ran its own tight loop. Each iteration of my game loop would deal with the state changes and interactions coming from each robot, synchronizing and managing it all. The following diagram shows what this architecture looks like:

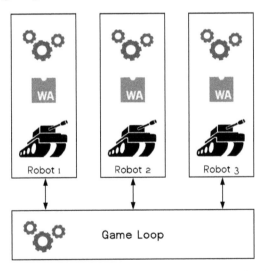

On the surface, it looks like this will do the job, but the devil is in the details, as they say. All we need is some kind of mutex that lets us block out other threads long enough for us to make our changes. Seems simple enough, right? Not quite. My first implementation of this literally ground to a halt. Even after

---

4. en.wikipedia.org/wiki/Game_programming#Game_structure

Rust's compiler blessed my code, my core game engine just continued to die in spectacular fashion, over and over again. In the next section, I'll explain why.

Entities, Components, and Systems

If you're not familiar with the concept of a *game loop*, it's fairly simple. This is a loop that's always running from the beginning of the match until the end. During each iteration of the loop, it takes care of maintenance of state and other actions.

The game loop in most games will do things like collision detection, inflicting damage, casting spells, depleting fuel from spaceships—all the housekeeping to keep all the individual parts of the game up to date. When I started working on this, I created a single struct called Robot that I figured could hold all that state that I need managed by the game loop. It looked something like this:

```
#[derive(Debug)]
pub struct Robot {
    pub player_name: String,
    pub damage: u32,
    pub status: DamageStatus,
    pub x: i32,
    pub y: i32,
    pub heading: i32,
    pub origin_x: i32,
    pub origin_y: i32,
    pub distance_on_heading: i32,
    pub speed: i32,
    pub desired_speed: i32,
    pub desired_heading: i32,
    pub accel: i32,
    pub last_scan_heading: i32,
    pub cannons: Vec&lt;Cannon&gt;
}
```

I took most of those fields from the original robot struct in Crobots.[5] If my game loop was the only thing that needed to manipulate that list of robots and their data, that would probably be fine. But the robots all need query access for their own data, and they have functions as part of the API that write values like desired heading and speed, and they perform actions like firing cannons.

This is where things went horribly wrong. Each iteration of my game loop would acquire a write lock on this list of robots because you can't acquire a write lock on just one element of a vector. It would then do all of the normal things and move on. Each thread from a running WebAssembly module would

---

5. github.com/tpoindex/crobots/blob/master/src/crobots.h#L30

then use a read lock on the entire vector and occasionally try and grab a write lock to modify a robot's data.

In this situation, the first thread that managed to get a write lock would ring the death bell for the rest of the app. If that thread was the game loop, it would only let go of it for such a short period of time (basically between the end and start of the `loop` block) and the loop would appear stalled, or the robots would stall. In some variants of this plan, *everything* stopped, and I felt like I had bitten off more than I could chew. Threading is hard. Shared mutable state is *super hard*, especially in Rust where you can't cheat. You can just "hope" you never have a data race.

The solution was to separate out the read concerns from the write concerns, and to narrow the focus of the write concerns down to as small a piece of state as possible. This is where the concept of *Entity—Component—System (ECS)*[6] comes in.

First and foremost, this pattern emphasizes *composition over inheritance*. Since we don't have classes with inheritance in Rust, this works out nicely. The real goal of ECS architecture is to separate concerns into small tiny pieces. Think of it as applying the microservices approach to a single piece of shared state. In my use of the ECS pattern in the game engine, I diverge from the core definition a little bit to keep the focus on the book and not on game design, but my heart is in the right place.

Entity
> Entities are just arbitrary things. In most ECS implementations, an entity is just some form of unique identifier and that's all. In our case, the entity will be the WebAssembly module name, which doubles as the player name.

Component
> A component is raw state for some aspect of an entity. A component labels an entity as "having a particular aspect." In our case, entities will have motion, damage, projectile, and scanner components.

System
> Systems perform logic and take action globally against components under their purview. In our engine, there's a system responsible for each component. In traditional ECS implementations, systems are often running in their own background threads, but I'm invoking mine sequentially to keep things as simple as I can while still building a functional game engine.

---

6.   en.wikipedia.org/wiki/Entity%E2%80%93component%E2%80%93system

With the concerns cut apart into components, and systems being the only things allowed to write to a component, we now have an architecture that can handle large amounts of concurrency without ever creating a situation where anyone is waiting on locks. Read locks are "free," and we can have as many of them active at a time as we want, but write locks are the ones that "stop the world," so to speak.

Now, in each iteration of the game loop, for example, the motion system can write to each of the motion components, advancing that component based on its speed, heading, acceleration, etc. The motion system doesn't care whether that component belongs to a player, a chair, or a doorknob. This narrow focus and division of responsibility is an elegant solution to concurrency that extends far beyond creating game engines with ECS, which is why I wanted to illustrate it in this chapter.

One potentially confusing aspect of a setup like this is that the robot API doesn't really *do* much. It makes requests by setting some desired state and then releasing the write lock, allowing the next pass of the relevant system to do the real work. As you'll see when you dig into the code, when a player launches a missile, the runtime just sets a missile status to ReadyToLaunch, and then the ProjectileSystem performs the actual launching of the missile the next time through the game loop.

Creating the Runtime Host

The first thing we need to do in order to pit WebAssembly robots against each other is load the modules and expose a Runtime for them. In previous chapters you saw how this works with the wasmi crate. Those implementations were pretty simple with only a function or two. Since we've got an entire API to support, we'll need to do a little bit of encapsulation and abstraction to keep the runtime clean.

Create a new library project beneath your workspace root called botengine (remember to also add this to your workspace Cargo.toml). Edit botengine's Cargo.toml to look like the following:

waros/botengine/Cargo.toml

```
[package]
name = "botengine"
version = "0.1.0"
authors = ["Your Email <your@mail.com>"]
edition = "2018"
```

```
[dependencies]
wasmi = "0.4.2"
rand = "0.6.1"
nalgebra = "0.16.11"
approx = "0.3.0"
```

Before we get into the runtime host, let's take a look at botengine/src/lib.rs. This is the root of the engine library, and it's where we're going to put the Combatant struct. The combatant is a wrapper around the loading, parsing, and interpreting of the WebAssembly module, as well as a start():

waros/botengine/src/lib.rs
```
use std::fmt;
use std::sync::Arc;
use std::thread;
use std::thread::JoinHandle;
use wasmi::{HostError, ImportsBuilder, Module, ModuleInstance, ModuleRef};

pub use crate::game::{GameState, Gameloop};
pub use crate::runtime::{Runtime, BOTINIT_NAME};

pub struct Combatant {}

impl Combatant {
    pub fn buffer_from_file(path: &str) -> Result<Vec<u8>> {
        use std::fs::File;
        use std::io::prelude::*;

        let mut file = File::open(path)?;
        let mut wasm_buf = Vec::new();
        let _bytes_read = file.read_to_end(&mut wasm_buf)?;
        Ok(wasm_buf)
    }
    pub fn start(
        name: &str,
        buffer: Vec<u8>,
➊       game_state: Arc<crate::game::GameState>,
➋   ) -> JoinHandle<()> {
        let n = name.to_string();

        thread::spawn(move || {
            let module = Module::from_buffer(&buffer).unwrap();
➌           let mut runtime = runtime::Runtime::init(game_state, n.clone());
            let moduleref =
                Self::get_module_instance_from_module(&module).unwrap();
➍           let res =
                moduleref.invoke_export(BOTINIT_NAME, &[][..], &mut runtime);
            println!("bot init loop exited for player {} - {:?}", n, res);
        })
    }
    fn get_module_instance_from_module(module: &Module) -> Result<ModuleRef> {
        let mut imports = ImportsBuilder::new();
        imports.push_resolver("env", &runtime::RuntimeModuleImportResolver);
```

```
        Ok(ModuleInstance::new(module, &imports)
            .expect("Failed to instantiate module")
            .assert_no_start())
    }
}
```

❶ The Arc (Atomically Reference Counted) is what lets us share pointers to the GameState struct.

❷ This function returns a JoinHandle but since the WebAssembly module is running an infinite loop, calling join() is likely to never return.

❸ Creates a new Runtime to host the WebAssembly module and passes it a reference to the game state.

❹ Invokes the bot_init() function in the WebAssembly module, starting the robot's infinite loop.

There are a couple of subtle things happening in this code. First, the Runtime is being instantiated *inside* the combatant's thread. This means the runtime doesn't need to cross thread boundaries, which makes the Rust compiler happy. There's also a clone happening of the player's name converting the &str into a String, letting us get away without having to use a lifetime specifier.

The rest of the lib.rs file contains implementations of various error handling traits, as is considered best practice when you're building a library you expect to expose to the rest of the world as a crate:

```
waros/botengine/src/lib.rs
/// A botengine error
#[derive(Debug)]
pub struct Error {
    kind: Kind,
}

/// Implements the wasmi HostError trait
impl HostError for Error {}

/// Implement standard error trait for the botengine error
impl std::error::Error for Error {
    fn description(&self) -> &str {
        "A botengine error ocurred"
    }

    fn cause(&self) -> Option<&std::error::Error> {
        None
    }
}
```

```rust
/// Ensure that the botengine error can be string formatted
impl fmt::Display for Error {
    fn fmt(&self, f: &mut fmt::Formatter) -> fmt::Result {
        match self.kind {
            Kind::InterpreterError(ref we) => fmt::Display::fmt(we, f),
            Kind::MiscFailure(ref s) => fmt::Display::fmt(s, f),
            Kind::IoError(ref s) => fmt::Display::fmt(s, f),
            Kind::ExportResolve(ref s) => fmt::Display::fmt(s, f),
        }
    }
}

/// Creates a botengine error from an I/O Error
impl From<std::io::Error> for Error {
    fn from(source: std::io::Error) -> Error {
        Error {
            kind: Kind::IoError(source),
        }
    }
}

impl From<wasmi::Error> for Error {
    fn from(source: wasmi::Error) -> Error {
        Error {
            kind: Kind::InterpreterError(source),
        }
    }
}

/// Indicates the kind of error that occurred.
#[derive(Debug)]
pub enum Kind {
    InterpreterError(wasmi::Error),
    IoError(std::io::Error),
    ExportResolve(String),
    MiscFailure(String),
}

/// A Result where failure is a botengine error
pub type Result<T> = std::result::Result<T, Error>;

mod events;
mod game;
mod runtime;
```

Next we need to implement the Runtime struct. We will put this in the botengine/src/runtime.rs file. This won't compile yet because the functions in the runtime all defer to code that's part of game state, components, or systems —all of which we'll discuss shortly. There's a lot of code here, and while I do enjoy typing, I wouldn't recommend trying to type this all in by hand. Save some time and just grab the whole source for this sample:

waros/botengine/src/runtime.rs
```rust
use crate::game::{readlock, scanner::ScannerSystem, writelock};
use crate::{Error, Kind};
use nalgebra::Point2;
use std::sync::Arc;
use wasmi::{
    Error as InterpreterError, Externals, FuncInstance, FuncRef,
    ModuleImportResolver, RuntimeArgs, RuntimeValue, Signature, Trap, ValueType,
};

/// Anchor struct for implementing the ModuleImportResolver trait
pub struct RuntimeModuleImportResolver;

/// Expose the list of host-provided functions, indexes, and signatures
/// to the WASM module(s) managed by this runtime
impl<'a> ModuleImportResolver for RuntimeModuleImportResolver {
    fn resolve_func(
        &self,
        field_name: &str,
        _signature: &Signature,
    ) -> Result<FuncRef, InterpreterError> {
        println!("Resolving {}", field_name);
        let func_ref = gen_funcref(field_name);
        match func_ref {
            Some(fr) => Ok(fr),
            None => Err(InterpreterError::Function(field_name.to_string())),
        }
    }
}

const SCAN_NAME: &'static str = "scan";
const SCAN_INDEX: usize = 0;
const CANNON_NAME: &'static str = "cannon";
const CANNON_INDEX: usize = 1;
const DRIVE_NAME: &'static str = "drive";
const DRIVE_INDEX: usize = 2;
const DAMAGE_NAME: &'static str = "damage";
const DAMAGE_INDEX: usize = 3;
const SPEED_NAME: &'static str = "speed";
const SPEED_INDEX: usize = 4;
const LOCX_NAME: &'static str = "loc_x";
const LOCX_INDEX: usize = 5;
const LOCY_NAME: &'static str = "loc_y";
const LOCY_INDEX: usize = 6;
const RAND_NAME: &'static str = "rand";
const RAND_INDEX: usize = 7;
const SQRT_NAME: &'static str = "wsqrt";
const SQRT_INDEX: usize = 8;
```

```rust
const SIN_NAME: &'static str = "wsin";
const SIN_INDEX: usize = 9;
const COS_NAME: &'static str = "wcos";
const COS_INDEX: usize = 10;
const TAN_NAME: &'static str = "wtan";
const TAN_INDEX: usize = 11;
const ATAN_NAME: &'static str = "watan";
const ATAN_INDEX: usize = 12;
const PLOT_COURSE_NAME: &'static str = "plot_course";
const PLOT_COURSE_INDEX: usize = 13;
pub const BOTINIT_NAME: &'static str = "botinit";

// Creates a FuncRef based on the name of the function
fn gen_funcref(name: &str) -> Option<FuncRef> {
    match name {
        SCAN_NAME => Some(FuncInstance::alloc_host(
            Signature::new(&[ValueType::I32, ValueType::I32][..],
                           Some(ValueType::I32)),
            SCAN_INDEX,
        )),
        CANNON_NAME => Some(FuncInstance::alloc_host(
            Signature::new(&[ValueType::I32, ValueType::I32][..],
                           Some(ValueType::I32)),
            CANNON_INDEX,
        )),
        DRIVE_NAME => Some(FuncInstance::alloc_host(
            Signature::new(&[ValueType::I32, ValueType::I32][..],
                           Some(ValueType::I32)),
            DRIVE_INDEX,
        )),
        DAMAGE_NAME => Some(FuncInstance::alloc_host(
            Signature::new(&[][..], Some(ValueType::I32)),
            DAMAGE_INDEX,
        )),
        SPEED_NAME => Some(FuncInstance::alloc_host(
            Signature::new(&[][..], Some(ValueType::I32)),
            SPEED_INDEX,
        )),
        LOCX_NAME => Some(FuncInstance::alloc_host(
            Signature::new(&[][..], Some(ValueType::I32)),
            LOCX_INDEX,
        )),
        LOCY_NAME => Some(FuncInstance::alloc_host(
            Signature::new(&[][..], Some(ValueType::I32)),
            LOCY_INDEX,
        )),
        RAND_NAME => Some(FuncInstance::alloc_host(
            Signature::new(&[ValueType::I32][..], Some(ValueType::I32)),
            RAND_INDEX,
        )),
```

```rust
            SQRT_NAME => Some(FuncInstance::alloc_host(
                Signature::new(&[ValueType::I32][..], Some(ValueType::I32)),
                SQRT_INDEX,
            )),
            SIN_NAME => Some(FuncInstance::alloc_host(
                Signature::new(&[ValueType::I32][..], Some(ValueType::I32)),
                SIN_INDEX,
            )),
            COS_NAME => Some(FuncInstance::alloc_host(
                Signature::new(&[ValueType::I32][..], Some(ValueType::I32)),
                COS_INDEX,
            )),
            TAN_NAME => Some(FuncInstance::alloc_host(
                Signature::new(&[ValueType::I32][..], Some(ValueType::I32)),
                TAN_INDEX,
            )),
            ATAN_NAME => Some(FuncInstance::alloc_host(
                Signature::new(&[ValueType::I32][..], Some(ValueType::I32)),
                ATAN_INDEX,
            )),
            PLOT_COURSE_NAME => Some(FuncInstance::alloc_host(
                Signature::new(&[ValueType::I32, ValueType::I32][..],
                        Some(ValueType::I32)),
                PLOT_COURSE_INDEX,
            )),
            _ => None,
        }
}

pub struct Runtime {
    pub game_state: Arc<super::game::GameState>,
    pub module_name: String,
    dead: bool,
}

impl Externals for Runtime {
    fn invoke_index(
        &mut self,
        index: usize,
        args: RuntimeArgs,
    ) -> Result<Option<RuntimeValue>, Trap> {
        match index {
            SCAN_INDEX => self.scan(args.nth(0), args.nth(1)),
            CANNON_INDEX => self.cannon(args.nth(0), args.nth(1)),
            DRIVE_INDEX => self.drive(args.nth(0), args.nth(1)),
            DAMAGE_INDEX => self.damage(),
            SPEED_INDEX => self.speed(),
            LOCX_INDEX => self.loc_x(),
            LOCY_INDEX => self.loc_y(),
            RAND_INDEX => self.rand(args.nth(0)),
            SQRT_INDEX => self.sqrt(args.nth(0)),
```

```
                SIN_INDEX => self.sin(args.nth(0)),
                COS_INDEX => self.cos(args.nth(0)),
                TAN_INDEX => self.tan(args.nth(0)),
                ATAN_INDEX => self.atan(args.nth(0)),
                PLOT_COURSE_INDEX => self.plot_course(args.nth(0), args.nth(1)),
                _ => Err(Trap::from(Error {
                    kind: Kind::MiscFailure("Invalid export index".to_string()),
                })),
            }
        }
    }
}

type WasmRuntimeResult = Result<Option<RuntimeValue>, Trap>;

impl Runtime {
    pub fn init(game_state: Arc<super::game::GameState>,
                module_name: String) -> Runtime {
        game_state.combatant_entered(&module_name);
        Runtime {
            game_state,
            module_name,
            dead: false,
        }
    }

    fn is_dead(&mut self) -> bool {
        if !self.dead {
            let dcs = self.game_state.damage_components.read().unwrap();
            let dc = dcs.get(&self.module_name);
            match dc {
                Some(d) => {
                    if let crate::game::damage::DamageStatus::Dead = d.status {
                        self.dead = true
                    }
                }
                None => {}
            }
        }

        self.dead
    }

    fn scan(&mut self, angle: i32, resolution: i32) -> WasmRuntimeResult {
        if self.is_dead() {
            return Ok(Some(RuntimeValue::from(-1)));
        }
        let angle = ScannerSystem::to_real_heading(angle);
        let resolution = (resolution as f32)
            .max(0.0)
            .min(super::game::scanner::RES_LIMIT);

        let degree = angle as f32;
```

```rust
        writelock(&self.game_state.scanner_components)
            .entry(self.module_name.to_string())
            .and_modify(|sc| sc.angle = degree as i32);

    let scan_result: i32 =
        ScannerSystem::scan(&self.game_state, &self.module_name,
                            degree, resolution);
    Ok(Some(RuntimeValue::from(ScannerSystem::to_user_heading(
        scan_result as f32,
    ))))
}

fn cannon(&mut self, angle: i32, range: i32) -> WasmRuntimeResult {
    if self.is_dead() {
        return Ok(Some(RuntimeValue::from(0)));
    }
    let angle = ScannerSystem::to_real_heading(angle);
    let mut launch_result = 0;
    let mc = &self.game_state.motion_components.read()
                .unwrap()[&self.module_name];

    writelock(&self.game_state.projectile_components)
        .entry(self.module_name.to_string())
        .and_modify(|pc| launch_result =
                    pc.launch(&mc.position, angle, range as u32));

    Ok(Some(RuntimeValue::from(launch_result)))
}

fn drive(&mut self, angle: i32, speed: i32) -> WasmRuntimeResult {
    if self.is_dead() {
        return Ok(Some(RuntimeValue::from(0)));
    }
    let angle = ScannerSystem::to_real_heading(angle);
    let speed = speed.min(super::game::motion::MAX_ENGINE);

    writelock(&self.game_state.motion_components)
        .entry(self.module_name.to_string())
        .and_modify(|mc| {
            mc.origin = mc.position.clone();
            mc.distance_along_heading = 0;
            mc.heading = angle;
            mc.desired_speed = speed;
        });

    Ok(Some(RuntimeValue::from(1_i32)))
}

fn damage(&mut self) -> WasmRuntimeResult {
    if self.is_dead() {
        return Ok(Some(RuntimeValue::from(100)));
    }
```

```rust
            Ok(
                match readlock(&self.game_state.damage_components)
                        .get(&self.module_name) {
                    Some(dc) => Some(RuntimeValue::from(dc.damage)),
                    None => None,
                },
            )
    }

    fn plot_course(&mut self, tx: i32, ty: i32) -> WasmRuntimeResult {
        if self.is_dead() {
            return Ok(Some(RuntimeValue::from(-1)));
        }
        Ok(
            match readlock(&self.game_state.motion_components)
                    .get(&self.module_name) {
                Some(mc) => {
                    let h = ScannerSystem::heading_to_target(
                        &mc.position,
                        &Point2::new(tx as f32, ty as f32),
                    );
                    Some(RuntimeValue::from(ScannerSystem::to_user_heading(h)))
                }
                None => None,
            },
        )
    }

    fn speed(&mut self) -> WasmRuntimeResult {
        if self.is_dead() {
            return Ok(Some(RuntimeValue::from(0)));
        }
        Ok(
            match readlock(&self.game_state.motion_components)
                    .get(&self.module_name) {
                Some(mc) => Some(RuntimeValue::from(mc.speed)),
                None => None,
            },
        )
    }

    fn loc_x(&mut self) -> WasmRuntimeResult {
        Ok(
            match readlock(&self.game_state.motion_components)
                    .get(&self.module_name) {
                Some(mc) => Some(RuntimeValue::from(mc.position.x as i32)),
                None => None,
            },
        )
    }
```

```rust
    fn loc_y(&mut self) -> WasmRuntimeResult {
        Ok(
            match readlock(&self.game_state.motion_components)
                    .get(&self.module_name) {
                Some(mc) => Some(RuntimeValue::from(mc.position.y as i32)),
                None => None,
            },
        )
    }

    fn rand(&mut self, limit: i32) -> WasmRuntimeResult {
        use rand::Rng;
        let mut rng = rand::thread_rng();
        let n: i32 = rng.gen_range(0, limit);

        Ok(Some(RuntimeValue::from(n)))
    }

    fn sqrt(&mut self, number: i32) -> WasmRuntimeResult {
        let val = (number as f32).sqrt();
        Ok(Some(RuntimeValue::from(val as i32)))
    }

    fn sin(&mut self, degree: i32) -> WasmRuntimeResult {
        Ok(Some(RuntimeValue::from(ScannerSystem::to_user_heading(
            (degree as f32).to_radians().sin(),
        ))))
    }

    fn cos(&mut self, degree: i32) -> WasmRuntimeResult {
        Ok(Some(RuntimeValue::from(ScannerSystem::to_user_heading(
            (degree as f32).to_radians().cos(),
        ))))
    }

    fn tan(&mut self, degree: i32) -> WasmRuntimeResult {
        Ok(Some(RuntimeValue::from(ScannerSystem::to_user_heading(
            (degree as f32).to_radians().tan(),
        ))))
    }

    fn atan(&mut self, degree: i32) -> WasmRuntimeResult {
        Ok(Some(RuntimeValue::from(ScannerSystem::to_user_heading(
            (degree as f32).to_radians().atan(),
        ))))
    }
}
```

In this file, the gen_funcref() function is one of the most important. This function takes as input the name of a function (one of the imports the WebAssembly modules expect the host to provide) and returns a function reference in the form of an Option<FuncRef>.

With the mapping between import name and import signature created, next we need to be able to call functions at the request of the modules. As you've seen before, we do this through the Externals trait. The invoke_index() function takes the index of a function (returned from our gen_funcref() function) and invokes it.

Finally, you get to the real meat of the Runtime—implementing the functions imported by WebAssembly modules. There's a *lot* of code here, but it all pretty much follows two basic patterns—reading from or writing to components. Occasionally we'll defer a call to a system to do a complex query, but that's an exception. Remember that the *systems* are the things tasked with processing, so these functions should do their work and get out of the way of the systems as quickly as possible. Let's take a look at the code to make a change to a component, like the code from drive():

```
writelock(&self.game_state.motion_components)
    .entry(self.module_name.to_string())
    .and_modify(|mc| {
        mc.origin = mc.position.clone();
        mc.distance_along_heading = 0;
        mc.heading = angle;
        mc.desired_speed = speed;
    });
```

The writelock() function (defined in the botengine/src/game/mod.rs file) creates a write lock on the self.game_state.motion_components HashMap. Then, the entry()[7] function is used to grab a reference to a single entry within the hash map. The Entry API is easily one of my favorites within all of Rust, and you owe it to yourself to learn it and exploit all of its power.

Anything inside the closure passed to and_modify() has safe, mutable access to the value within that entry. In this case, it's a single motion component and we modify it to set a new heading, reset its distance along that heading to 0, and set the desired speed.

The code to read a value from a component looks similar:

```
match readlock(&self.game_state.damage_components).get(&self.module_name) {
    Some(dc) => Some(RuntimeValue::from(dc.damage)),
    None => None,
}
```

Here the readlock() function (also a utility defined elsewhere) grabs a read lock on the damage_components HashMap. Instead of calling entry(), we use get() here and

---

7. doc.rust-lang.org/std/collections/hash_map/enum.Entry.html

match on the result. As long as no other thread is writing to damage_components at that moment, acquiring a read lock is free.

Implementing the Game Loop

The *game loop* is the core gear that makes everything else in the game work. Without it, nothing happens. The job of this loop is to tell each of the active systems to apply its logic. The loop also keeps track of the number of loops or "cycles" that have occurred. When we discuss replay, you'll see why this is important.

In more formal ECS frameworks, each system might be operating in its own loop, so you have a bunch of miniature game loops rather than a single all-encompassing one. I opted for the single loop here to keep the sample easier to read and to help with playback:

```
waros/botengine/src/game/mod.rs
use self::damage::*;
use self::motion::*;
use self::projectiles::*;
use self::scanner::*;
use crate::events::GameEvent;
use std::collections::HashMap;
use std::sync::{mpsc::Sender, Arc, RwLock};
use std::sync::{RwLockReadGuard, RwLockWriteGuard};

pub struct Gameloop {
    game_state: Arc<GameState>,
    systems: Vec<Box<System>>,
    cycle: u32,
    max_cycles: u32,
    num_combatants: usize,
}

#[derive(Debug)]
pub enum LoopTerminationReason {
    CycleCountExceeded,
}

pub trait System {
    fn apply(self: &Self, cycle: u32, game_state: &Arc<GameState>);
}

impl Gameloop {
    pub fn new(
        game_state: Arc<GameState>,
        max_cycles: u32,
        num_combatants: usize,
        logger: Option<Sender<GameEvent>>,
    ) -> Gameloop {
        Gameloop {
```

```
                game_state,
                systems: vec![
                    Box::new(ScannerSystem::new(logger.clone())),
                    Box::new(MotionSystem::new(logger.clone())),
                    Box::new(ProjectileSystem::new(logger.clone())),
                    Box::new(DamageSystem::new(logger.clone())),
                ],
                cycle: 0,
                max_cycles,
                num_combatants,
            }
        }

    pub fn start(&mut self) -> LoopTerminationReason {
        loop {
            self.systems
                .iter()
                .for_each(|s| s.apply(self.cycle, &self.game_state));

            self.cycle = self.cycle + 1;

            if self.cycle >= self.max_cycles {
                return LoopTerminationReason::CycleCountExceeded;
            }
        }
    }
}
```

The GameLoop struct's new() function takes an Arc of the GameState, number of combatants, and a Sender as initial arguments. The Arc is used to allow code to pass multiple safe references to the same source object.

The core loop is very simple—iterate through each system and invoke its apply() function. You'll see a few of those in the next section. Let's take a look at how the game state is defined:

```
waros/botengine/src/game/mod.rs
pub type ReadWriteLocked<T> = Arc<RwLock<T>>;
pub type ComponentHash<T> = ReadWriteLocked<HashMap<String, T>>;

#[derive(Debug)]
pub struct GameState {
    pub players: ReadWriteLocked<Vec<String>>,
    pub motion_components: ComponentHash<MotionComponent>,
    pub damage_components: ComponentHash<DamageComponent>,
    pub scanner_components: ComponentHash<ScannerComponent>,
    pub projectile_components: ComponentHash<ProjectileComponent>,
}

impl GameState {
    pub fn new() -> GameState {
        GameState {
            players: Arc::new(RwLock::new(Vec::new())),
```

```rust
                motion_components: Arc::new(RwLock::new(HashMap::new())),
                damage_components: Arc::new(RwLock::new(HashMap::new())),
                scanner_components: Arc::new(RwLock::new(HashMap::new())),
                projectile_components: Arc::new(RwLock::new(HashMap::new())),
            }
        }

    pub fn combatant_entered(&self, module_name: &str) {
        self.players.write().unwrap().push(module_name.to_string());
        self.motion_components
            .write()
            .unwrap()
            .entry(module_name.to_string())
            .or_insert(MotionComponent::new());
        self.damage_components
            .write()
            .unwrap()
            .entry(module_name.to_string())
            .or_insert(DamageComponent::new());
        self.scanner_components
            .write()
            .unwrap()
            .entry(module_name.to_string())
            .or_insert(ScannerComponent::new());
        self.projectile_components
            .write()
            .unwrap()
            .entry(module_name.to_string())
            .or_insert(ProjectileComponent::new());
    }
}

pub fn readlock<'a, T>(
    component: &'a ComponentHash<T>
) -> RwLockReadGuard<'a, HashMap<String, T>> {
    component.read().unwrap()
}

pub fn writelock<'a, T>(
    component: &'a ComponentHash<T>,
) -> RwLockWriteGuard<'a, HashMap<String, T>> {
    component.write().unwrap()
}

const MAX_X: f32 = 1000.0;
const MAX_Y: f32 = 1000.0;

pub mod damage;
pub mod motion;
mod projectiles;
pub mod scanner;
```

First I use a couple of type aliases to keep the "bracket noise" down when nesting generic type parameters in the upcoming function signatures and structs. Each system has a corresponding ComponentHash, which is a HashMap wrapped by a RwLock and an Arc. In other words, the game state holds an atomically reference counted read-write lock on a hash map for each component.

In the combatant_entered() function, each of the HashMaps is updated to contain a new default entry for the new player. Remember when I said the Entry API was incredibly powerful? Here it is again:

```
self.motion_components
  .write()
  .unwrap()
  .entry(module_name.to_string())
  .or_insert(MotionComponent::new());
```

We can skip the usual ugliness with if statements or pattern matches to check for the existence of an item and just use the or_insert() function to insert a new entry if one doesn't already exist.

Next, we have what might be considered the most complex Rust syntax that I've used in the book so far:

```
pub fn writelock<'a, T>(component: &'a ComponentHash<T>) ->
  RwLockWriteGuard<'a, HashMap<String, T>> {
  component.write().unwrap()
}
```

All I've done is create a shortcut (I could also have used a macro) for calling .write().unwrap(). Every single access to every component for every system required the use of the RwLock methods, and I got tired of typing them all of the time.

This function signature includes a lifetime specifier ('a) and a generic type parameter (T). Without getting into too many gory details, this code indicates that the returned RwLockWriteGuard must last as long as the component passed in as a parameter. We use generics here so we can get a RwLockWriteGuard on any of the component HashMaps, even though each map contains values of different types.

Building the Components and Systems

As we went over earlier, a component is a small, discrete piece of state. A system is some set of logic that operates on that state. The separation of components and systems makes code easier to test, and the smaller surface area over which write locks need to be acquired help reduce the risk of "wait blocks" in the game loop.

I won't show the code for each system in the interest of saving a few trees (and bytes). You can download all of the engine code and check out each system on your own. With a few exceptions, most of the system implementations try and mimic the behavior and spirit of Poindexter's original Crobots code. Let's take a look at the core of the damage system:

waros/botengine/src/game/damage.rs
```
use super::*;
use crate::events::log_event;
use crate::game::{readlock, writelock};

pub struct DamageSystem {
    logger: Option<Sender<GameEvent>>,
}

impl System for DamageSystem {
    fn apply(&self, cycle: u32, game_state: &Arc<GameState>) {
        game_state.players.read().unwrap().iter().for_each(|p| {
            writelock(&game_state.damage_components)
                .entry(p.to_string())
                .and_modify(|dc| self.advance(p, game_state, dc, cycle));
        });
    }
}
```

The apply() function will mutate a damage component for each player in the game by calling the damage system's advance() function on that mutable reference, acquired from a write lock. Since the damage system is ideally the only part of the game that mutates damage components, we don't have to worry about blocking other threads to perform these quick mutations.

There is a "breadcrumb" pattern used by multiple systems in the game. Each system sets some value at the end of its apply() loop, leaving it behind to be used by other systems that process next. For example, the collision system leaves values in the collision components indicating detected collisions *during that game loop cycle*.

The damage system just reads any active collisions and applies damage accordingly. It's responsible for ensuring that detected collisions only last as long as they should. For example, explosion damage from projectiles actually last a few cycles (also called "ticks"), which means the damage system may apply damage multiple times per explosion.

Let's take a look at the rest of the code for the damage system to see how it applies collision damage, projectile damage, and then checks to see if players are dead:

waros/botengine/src/game/damage.rs

```rust
impl DamageSystem {
  pub fn new(logger: Option<Sender<GameEvent>>) -> DamageSystem {
    DamageSystem { logger }
  }

  pub fn advance(
    &self,
    player: &str,
    game_state: &Arc<GameState>,
    dc: &mut DamageComponent,
    cycle: u32,
  ) {
    self.apply_collision_damage(player, game_state, dc, cycle);
    self.apply_projectile_damage(player, game_state, dc, cycle);
    self.check_death(player, dc, cycle);
  }
  fn check_death(&self, player: &str, dc: &mut DamageComponent, cycle: u32) {
    if dc.damage >= DAMAGE_MAX && !dc.dead() {
      dc.damage = DAMAGE_MAX;
      dc.status = DamageStatus::Dead;
      log_event(
        &self.logger,
        GameEvent::Death {
          cycle,
          victim: player.to_string(),
        },
      );
    }
  }
  fn apply_collision_damage(
    &self,
    player: &str,
    game_state: &Arc<GameState>,
    dc: &mut DamageComponent,
    cycle: u32,
  ) {
    let mcs = readlock(&game_state.motion_components);
    let mc_opt = mcs.get(player);
    match mc_opt {
      Some(mc) => match mc.collision {
        Some(CollisionType::Player(ref p)) => {
          dc.add_damage(DAMAGE_COLLISION);
          self.log_damage(
            cycle,
            DAMAGE_COLLISION,
            DamageKind::Collision(
             CollisionType::Player(p.to_string())),
            player,
          );
        }
```

```rust
        Some(CollisionType::Wall(ref p)) => {
          dc.add_damage(DAMAGE_COLLISION);
          self.log_damage(
            cycle,
            DAMAGE_COLLISION,
            DamageKind::Collision(CollisionType::Wall(p.clone())),
            player,
          );
        }
        None => {}
      },
      None => {}
    }
  }
  fn apply_projectile_damage(
    &self,
    player: &str,
    game_state: &Arc<GameState>,
    dc: &mut DamageComponent,
    cycle: u32,
  ) {
    let pcs = game_state.projectile_components.read().unwrap();
    let pc_opt = pcs.get(player);
    match pc_opt {
      Some(pc) => {
        for x in 0..1 {
          if pc.projectiles[x].active_hits.contains_key(player) {
            let dmg: u32 = pc.projectiles[x].active_hits[player];
            println!("Doing explosion damage {} to player {}", dmg, player);
            dc.add_damage(dmg);
            self.log_damage(cycle, dmg, DamageKind::Projectile, player);
          }
        }
      }
      None => {}
    }
  }
  fn log_damage(&self, cycle: u32, amount: u32, kind: DamageKind,
        victim: &str) {
    log_event(
      &self.logger,
      GameEvent::Damage {
        cycle,
        amount,
        kind,
        victim: victim.to_string(),
      },
    );
  }
}
```

```rust
#[derive(Debug)]
pub enum DamageStatus {
    Alive,
    Dead,
}

#[derive(Debug)]
pub struct DamageComponent {
    pub damage: u32,
    pub status: DamageStatus,
}

#[derive(Debug)]
pub enum DamageKind {
    Collision(CollisionType),
    Projectile,
}

impl DamageComponent {
    pub fn new() -> DamageComponent {
        DamageComponent {
            damage: 0,
            status: DamageStatus::Alive,
        }
    }

    pub fn dead(&self) -> bool {
        match self.status {
            DamageStatus::Dead => true,
            _ => false,
        }
    }

    fn add_damage(&mut self, amount: u32) {
        self.damage += amount; // death will be checked end of this tick
    }
}

const DAMAGE_COLLISION: u32 = 2;
pub const DAMAGE_MAX: u32 = 100;
```

The logger you've seen in the game loop and the damage system helps support playback, which we'll discuss next.

Supporting Match Playback

The game engine's loop runs as fast as it possibly can. This is fine for when we just want to determine who will win the match. But what if we want to watch the match live, or watch a replay of the match? To facilitate this, I'm using a Sender[8] to send important game events bound to the cycle/frame

---

8. doc.rust-lang.org/std/sync/mpsc/struct.Sender.html

during which those events occurred. Anything listening on the other end of that channel can store the events in a database, display them on the console, or render them on a website. To show them at a more human-friendly speed, just apply a frame rate delay between events such that each cycle represents some fixed fraction of a second.

Creating WebAssembly Robots

Now for the fun part: creating WebAssembly robots! We've built an engine that can load WebAssembly modules into memory, expose a runtime host for them, and safely allow them to interact with a virtual environment and manipulate shared state. Now it's time to exercise that engine by building some robots.

First, let's create a fairly dumb target. I wanted a "read hungry" robot to ensure that no matter how frequently a robot queried its own state, it couldn't cause a threading dead lock in the system. Create a new library Rust module called dumbotrs and add it to the workspace. Its Cargo.toml should look like the following:

waros/dumbotrs/Cargo.toml
```
[package]
name = "dumbotrs"
version = "0.1.0"
authors = ["Your Name <your@mail.com>"]

[lib]
crate-type = ["cdylib"]

[dependencies]
warsdk = { path = "../warsdk" }
```

This robot only depends on the SDK we created earlier that exposes the host functions. Let's take a look at lib.rs:

waros/dumbotrs/src/lib.rs
```
extern crate warsdk;
use warsdk::*;

#[no_mangle]
pub extern "C" fn botinit() -> i32 {
    drive(90, 10);

    loop {
        damage();
        speed();
    }
}
```

This robot, regardless of its starting position, drives north at a speed of 10%. It then goes into an infinite loop where it continually queries its own state. This robot should eventually collide with the northern wall and stop, where it will keep eagerly consuming its state.

Since we will probably never need to compile this robot for anything other than the wasm32-unknown-unknown target, we can tell Cargo to default to that by creating a .cargo/config file inside the project directory:

waros/dumbotrs/.cargo/config
```
[build]
target = "wasm32-unknown-unknown"
```

Creating the Rook

The Rook, inspired by Poindexter's original implementation,[9] is a robot that seeks the middle of the game board. Once there, it will move laterally east and west, scanning for potential targets at the four compass points. Once it finds one, it stops and fires at it until there are no more targets in range.

This is a subtle yet fairly powerful strategy. If an opposing robot is anywhere but the extreme top or bottom of the game board, it will eventually be detected by the rook's scanners and fired upon. The only escape is to keep moving or to kill the rook.

Create a new library Rust project called rook, add it to the workspace, and set its default compilation target to wasm32-unknown-unknown. Update its Cargo.toml to include a relative path dependency on the warsdk code. Let's take a look at what the rook looks like written in Rust:

waros/rook/src/lib.rs
```rust
/* Inspired by https://github.com/tpoindex/crobots/blob/master/src/rook.r
 *
 * Will move to the center of the field and then patrol from East to West,
 * scanning all four compass points for targets. If it is hit while scanning
 * it will change direction
 *
 * Note: this rook ignores incoming fire while on its way to the center of the
 * battlefield.
 */
extern crate warsdk;
use warsdk::*;

struct State {
    course: i32,
}
```

---

9. github.com/tpoindex/crobots/blob/master/src/rook.r

```rust
#[no_mangle]
pub extern "C" fn botinit() -> i32 {
    go(500, 500);

    let mut state = State { course: 0 };

    loop {
        look(ANGLE_EAST, &mut state);
        look(ANGLE_NORTH, &mut state);
        look(ANGLE_WEST, &mut state);
        look(ANGLE_SOUTH, &mut state);

        if loc_x() > BOUND_X_MAX {
            reverse(&mut state);
        }

        if loc_x() < BOUND_X_MIN {
            reverse(&mut state);
        }

        if speed() == 0 {
            // bumped into something
            reverse(&mut state);
        }
    }
}

fn look(angle: i32, state: &mut State) {
    let mut range = scan(angle, 2);

    // Fire at targets in range until we have no targets in range
    while range > 0 && range < PROJECTILE_MAX_RANGE as i32 {
        if speed() > 0 {
            drive(state.course, 0);
        }

        if range > BLAST_RADIUS {
            // don't want to blow ourselves up!
            cannon(angle, range);
        }
        range = scan(angle, 2);
    }
}

fn reverse(state: &mut State) {
    if state.course == ANGLE_EAST {
        state.course = ANGLE_WEST;
    } else {
        state.course = ANGLE_EAST;
    }
}

const BOUND_X_MIN: i32 = 80;
const BOUND_X_MAX: i32 = 920;
```

In this robot's implementation, you can see we now have our own internal, mutable state. This is a really powerful capability, because it means that the robots can make complex decisions based on observations from previous iterations through their loops. In the case of the rook, it maintains the direction it's facing so it can reverse it when it reaches a boundary near the eastern or western edges of the game board.

Cry Havoc, and Let Slip the Robots of War!

You've got a game engine, and you've got a couple of robots (as well as a couple included in the code not listed in the chapter). It's time to pit them against each other and see what happens. To do this, we'll create another project in the workspace called consolerunner, a CLI application that loads wasm modules and invokes the engine:

```
waros/consolerunner/src/main.rs
extern crate botengine;
use botengine::{Combatant, Gameloop};
use std::sync::mpsc::channel;
use std::sync::Arc;
use std::thread;
use std::time;

fn main() {
    let gs = Arc::new(botengine::GameState::new());

    let b1 = botengine::Combatant::buffer_from_file(
        "./bots/dumbotrs.wasm");
    let bot1 = b1.unwrap();

    let b2 = botengine::Combatant::buffer_from_file(
        "./bots/rook.wasm");
    let bot2 = b2.unwrap();

    let rb = botengine::Combatant::buffer_from_file(
        "./bots/rabbit.wasm");
    let rabbit = rb.unwrap();

    let my_gs = gs.clone();
    let debug_gs = gs.clone();

    let (sender, receiver) = channel();
    thread::spawn(move || loop {
        match receiver.recv() {
            Ok(ge) => println!("{:?}", ge),
            Err(_) => {}
        }
    });

    let mut gl = Gameloop::new(my_gs, 100_000, 3, Some(sender));

    let _handle = Combatant::start("bot-1", bot1, gs.clone());
```

```
let _handle2 = Combatant::start("rook", bot2, gs.clone());
let _handle3 = Combatant::start("rabbit", rabbit, gs.clone());
let game_result = gl.start();

thread::sleep(time::Duration::from_secs(1));

println!(
    "Game loop terminated: {:?}\nState: {:?}",
    game_result, debug_gs
);
}
```

This code loads three robots from the bots directory (the files were just copied from target output of other modules), creates the GameState, and shares clones of the Arc of that state with instances of the Combatant struct.

When all is ready to go, we invoke start() on the game loop and wait for the match to resolve after 100,000 frames or cycles. You'll also see that I've created a channel and set up a thread where I await events in an infinite loop. This prints them to the console, but you can imagine a whole host of other things we could do with the list of game events.

Run the application either by compiling and running the binary or simply with cargo run. You'll see a ton of spam that comes from the rook as it launches missiles at the rabbit as the rabbit bounces randomly across the game field. Since the rabbit never spends more than a single frame sitting in a spot, it *usually* manages to escape every match almost completely unharmed, save for a few unfortunate collisions with walls. Poor dumbotrs heads north, hits a wall, incurs two points of damage, and then spends the rest of the match idle.

Congratulations! You now have a fully functioning game engine inspired by the original Crobots that pits multiple WebAssembly modules against each other. This can be used to teach people how to write Rust WebAssembly modules as well as for a lot of fun and senseless virtual battlefield violence, and to illustrate how to allocate dedicated threads to WebAssembly host runtimes.

Room for Improvement

There's plenty more that you could do with this game engine. Most of it, however, has little to do with WebAssembly itself. You could add a new system and component pair that allocates points to players every time they do damage to another player. You could then create yet another system and component pair that can declare victory and terminate a match early when only a single robot is left standing.

I hope you will see places where you can have fun improving this code to continue learning Rust and WebAssembly.

Robots in the Cloud

The WARoS engine is deliberately designed as a module that you can use from any kind of code. If this were published as a public crate on crates.io, you could declare a dependency on it in any application you're writing and immediately gain the ability to run multi-player WebAssembly combat matches on demand.

If you wanted to expose this as a cloud offering, you're only a few steps away. You could build a website that allows developers to upload their own robot modules, and then the website could hold randomly chosen matches between stored robots. If you wanted to get really fancy, you could create a logger (just a Receiver half of a channel) that, instead of displaying events to the console, emits them to a message broker like NATS, RabbitMQ, or Kafka. You could then have a web page listening on web sockets for events, rendering matches in real time for live spectators.

The possibilities are endless—leader boards, competitions, prizes, achievements, even different kinds of battlefields with obstacles and barriers other than simple walls at the edge. I would love to spend months coding all of that, but this book is about WebAssembly, so I (and my editor) had to draw the line somewhere.

If you're as into distributed systems as I am, one could even imagine a cluster in which a match execution service had been deployed, awaiting signals from a message broker to begin a match. As a match begins, it emits events back to the broker, which could be listened to by a scribe service (recording matches for posterity), a projector service (updating live state of each robot and match), and to a real-time spectator service responsible for delivering updates on matches straight to browser clients.

Wrapping Up

This chapter was arguably the most "rusty" of the chapters. There were a number of core lessons at the heart of this chapter and are the reason for the relatively large amount of code. If you only scratch the surface of Rust, you'll never fully take advantage of its true power.

In this chapter, first and foremost, you saw an example of how to hide tremendous complexity behind a simple API—the host functions available to the robots in your virtual arena. Next, you saw how to manage complex, shared access to both mutable and immutable data. Finally, you explored some of Rust's intrinsic support for threads. There are frameworks out there with simpler APIs, but knowing the standard library implementation is invaluable.

The code for this chapter also provides a foundation for further exploration. If you want, you can add things like obstacles in the arena, you can allow players to choose from a variety of weapons instead of giving them all the same gear, you can play with the motion system or convert the whole thing from robots to space ships or dragons.

Conclusion

Throughout this book, you've been on a journey. You've started at the very basics and foundations of WebAssembly, learning what it is, what it isn't, and what you can do with it even at the lowest levels writing wat code directly.

From there you learned about how WebAssembly and JavaScript can interact, from the foundational levels of low-level interop to the use of high-level code generation tools that do everything from wrap the JavaScript APIs to expose full-featured, React-like web application development frameworks.

You then took the next step in that journey, learning how to host WebAssembly modules within Rust itself for everything from running a checkers game in the console to controlling LEDs on a Raspberry Pi. And now, you've put every ounce of that journey to work for you in order to create a reusable game engine capable of allocating dedicated threads to WebAssembly modules as their internal code navigates the hazards of a virtual battlefield that can be hosted in a console, on the web, in the cloud, or anywhere else.

Hopefully the next step in this journey will involve you continuing to explore, experiment with, and learn from, the combination of the Rust programming language and the emerging and game-changing WebAssembly standard. Nothing would make me happier than hearing about all of the great projects started after being inspired by this book. You should take what you've learned in this book and explore, fail, learn, and find the next amazing thing to build, no matter how big or small.

WebAssembly and Serverless

If you've been keeping up with your home game of "buzzword bingo," then you've undoubtedly heard of the latest and greatest thing that claims to solve all of our problems—*serverless*. Since serverless is a topic that already has multiple books on its own, I didn't want to derail the main journey of the book with a lengthy digression on it.

However, I think it's important to provide some discussion and perspective around what serverless is, with the hype stripped away, and how WebAssembly development might fit into that rapidly expanding area of innovation.

Serverless 101

Serverless may be more popular on the Internet for those exclaiming, "serverless still has servers!" than for the actual concept. Stripped from the hype, my own view of serverless is that as we continue to build smaller and smaller components, designed to elastically scale and conform to all of the standards for cloud native development, we reach a point where we start to see a pattern emerging.

In this pattern, we start off a microservice with a stack of boilerplate. This boilerplate is responsible for standing up a server, exposing an endpoint—be it REST or RPC or pub/sub or whatever—securing and routing requests to the business logic, responding to callers with some standardized serialized payload. This boilerplate can also include logging, application monitoring, tracing, security, fault tolerance, ad nauseum.

What we often see is that as our services get smaller, so too do the core bits of business logic. At some point we notice that we've got more boilerplate than "real code." When you have hundreds of services in many different clusters and they're all running duplicated in multiple availability zones, this boilerplate starts to look like a lot of unecessary overhead.

The way I view serverless is that it takes the core function out of the service and then defers all of the other requirements previously managed by duplicated boilerplate to the platform, which is in most cases a cloud provider or some abstraction within a cluster like OpenFaaS (I will talk about that shortly). Serverless is also *reactive*—a serverless function, stripped of its surrounding onion of boilerplate, awaits an event, performs a task, and gets out of the way.

If you're still a little fuzzy on the subject, I highly recommend searching for blog posts, use cases, and case studies on when and where serverless is an ideal solution, rather than the technology behind individual serverless implementations like AWS Lambda or Google Cloud Functions.

Intersection of WebAssembly and Serverless

Now that we're all on the same page with the idea that serverless is just event-driven functions with their ceremonial robes of non-functional requirements delegated to a platform abstraction, let's talk about what any of that has to do with WebAssembly.

After reading this book, hopefully your perspective on what WebAssembly is and how it can be harnessed has changed. A WebAssembly module is a portable encapsulation of some set of functionality. Where it begins to intersect with serverless is that on their own, WebAssembly modules are helpless. It cannot make HTTP requests from inside a module without an explicit contract with the host allowing it to do so, it can't listen on endpoints unless the host lets it do it. By and large, WebAssembly modules are *more* limited than regular serverless functions—and that's a good thing.

As you've seen in this book, if you write your WebAssembly code in a way that conforms to a well-known host interface (like the one provided by a compliant web browser), then your code is truly portable. It can run anywhere that contract is satisfied, whether that's a Raspberry Pi, a Rust console application, a web browser, or a *serverless platform* like the ones I'll discuss next.

WebAssembly in the Cloud

Every big cloud provider today has some form of support for serverless computing, or "cloud functions." They each have their own name for it, and each one of the providers tries to add value in their own unique way to convince customers that their function hosting is better than everyone else's. Amazon

AWS has Lambda,[1] Google Cloud Platform has Google Cloud Functions,[2] Microsoft has Azure Functions,[3] and Alibaba Cloud has Function Compute.[4]

To the best of my knowledge, none of these serverless platforms has any kind of native support for WebAssembly—yet. I am hopeful that by the end of 2019, at least one of the major providers will allow for some kind of native integration of WebAssembly modules into cloud functions. Just the binary portability alone makes this an appealing offering. Some providers may be waiting for the host interface to get a little more robust (e.g., to allow native string passing so there wouldn't have to be explicit allocation calls in the host contract).

Today, Amazon Lambda supports a Rust runtime for functions. This means you could take the Rust WebAssembly host code examples from this book and write a host that consumes JSON events, converts them into something suitable for the hosted module, and invokes a function. Is this really worth the overhead, though? Do we actually gain any benefit from creating another nested layer within a cloud function?

In some cases it might be useful. Given the limited abilities of a WebAssembly module, they become notably easier to test. For example, a JavaScript function that makes external HTTP requests would require complicated mocks, injection, or standing up a fake server to test properly. But if the WebAssembly module just invoked a make_http_request() function, then a test harness for that module could easily fake it. Whether this additional degree of indirection is worth it depends on you, your development team, and of course the problem you're trying to solve. This scenario does gain a bit more traction when you plan on running the same logic both inside and outside of the serverless platform.

As the WebAssembly specification grows and the community of developers creating Wasm-based solutions also grows, I expect a lot of people to notice the potential of combining WebAssembly's performance, security, and portability with the flexibility and cost-effectiveness of cloud functions.

Serverless WebAssembly in the Wild

There are a number of projects available now where people are experimenting with serverless WebAssembly in one form or another. For example, Geoffrey Couprie has written serverless-wasm,[5] a framework that starts up an HTTP

---

1. aws.amazon.com/lambda
2. cloud.google.com/functions
3. azure.microsoft.com/en-us/services/functions
4. www.alibabacloud.com/product/function-compute
5. github.com/Geal/serverless-wasm

server and, through a toml configuration file, can route HTTP requests to different wasm modules. The host contract for this framework looks like this (at the time this book was finished):

```
mod sys {
    extern {
        pub fn log(ptr: *const u8, size: u64);
        pub fn response_set_status_line(status: u32, ptr: *const u8, size: u64);
        pub fn response_set_header(name_ptr: *const u8, name_size: u64,
            value_ptr: *const u8, value_size: u64);
        pub fn response_set_body(ptr: *const u8, size: u64);
        pub fn tcp_connect(ptr: *const u8, size: u64) -> i32;
        pub fn tcp_read(fd: i32, ptr: *mut u8, size: u64) -> i64;
        pub fn tcp_write(fd: i32, ptr: *const u8, size: u64) -> i64;
        pub fn db_get(key_ptr: *const u8, key_size: u64,
            value_ptr: *const u8, value_size: u64) -> i64;
    }
}
```

This framework allows WebAssembly modules to read and write over raw TCP connections as well as make connections to a database back-end. As I mentioned earlier, this contract can be satisfied by anything, including a mock host which makes testing these modules fairly easy. It's up to you whether you decide to let your modules make external connections.

Colin Eberhardt takes a different approach in his blog post,[6] where the WebAssembly function written in Rust is hosted in AWS's NodeJS Lambda runtime. This is certainly a far simpler way to host a WebAssembly module than trying to manipulate all of the lower-level Rust APIs you've seen in this book to host a module. Using NodeJS as the host runtime means the Rust WebAssembly module developer can take advantage of wasm-bindgen, making it even easier to write modules.

Yet another option available for serverless WebAssembly is the use of *Cloudflare Workers*. They just recently announced support for WebAssembly workers[7] and you can use the wasm-pack tool to bundle up your WebAssembly code and deploy it to Cloudflare, as illustrated in their blog post[8] covering the subject. This support is still JavaScript-based, so it resembles using a NodeJS runtime in AWS to invoke a WebAssembly module, but this is definitely an indication that the future of serverless WebAssembly is a bright one.

---

6. blog.scottlogic.com/2018/10/18/serverless-rust.html
7. https://blog.cloudflare.com/webassembly-on-cloudflare-workers
8. blog.cloudflare.com/cloudflare-workers-as-a-serverless-rust-platform/

Integration with OpenFaaS

OpenFaaS[9] (Open Functions as a Service) takes a different approach to cloud functions. Where the major cloud providers implement all of the underlying infrastructure for you, OpenFaaS expects you to have that infrastructure available (which could still be AWS, GCP, Azure, etc).

There could be full books written about OpenFaaS as well, so I will try and keep my explanation brief. Unlike the other cloud providers which have different runtimes for each language, OpenFaaS has a single runtime for all functions—*docker* and the deployed OpenFaas components.

In OpenFaaS, your function is a compiled binary inside a docker image. This docker image also contains a *watchdog* process that acts as a proxy between the OpenFaaS gateway and your function. It routes incoming requests for function invocations to your process. The classic gateway communication mode is about as simple as it gets: the request payload is conveyed to your process via stdin and your response is delivered via stdout. There's also a newer watchdog type[10] that's faster and uses HTTP.

So while your function process is just a simple binary, OpenFaaS takes care of waking it up and invoking it on demand and deals with the complexities of trying to keep it "warm," and so on. You could also use a WebAssembly module here. All you'd need is a host process (e.g. a Rust application) that conformed to any of the OpenFaaS watchdog requirements and you could quickly turn your WebAssembly module into a function that could be launched on-demand in a Kubernetes cluster hosted wherever you like.

In this scenario, you could also reap the benefits of knowing the WebAssembly module could never do anything to harm your cluster or OpenFaaS, because the host is in complete control of what the module can and cannot do. You can even verify that the module was deployed by the right people or services —the subject of this book's second appendix.

---

9. www.openfaas.com
10. docs.openfaas.com/architecture/watchdog

Securing WebAssembly Modules

I devoted the vast majority of the book to illustrating how WebAssembly modules can be created, hosted, consumed, and integrated. What I didn't talk about was, once you've got a WebAssembly module, what are the security concerns and how do you mitigate them?

This appendix will briefly mention a few things that you should keep in mind when considering the security implications of using WebAssembly. It is by no means an exhaustive reference or guide.

General Security Concerns

The most basic security concern with WebAssembly modules you saw in the "round-trip" compilation sample early on in the book. Anything that you compile into a wasm file can be disassembled and converted back into wast text format, or even other languages capable of targeting WebAssembly.

This means that you should never believe that anything in your module will remain private. Nor should you ever put anything into the WebAssembly module that could be considered a trade secret. In other words, if you wouldn't want it exposed to the public, don't put it in a WebAssembly module. This is essentially the same advice given to people writing client-side JavaScript. We've got obfuscation and minimization tools, but if someone wants to reverse engineer your logic, they'll do it.

Browser-Based Attack Vectors

Internally, WebAssembly has a number of features[1] that keep it fairly secure. It has sandboxed memory and a number of common ways of attacking code

---

1. webassembly.org/docs/security

like forcing invalid jumps or corrupting memory don't happen inside a WebAssembly sandbox.

That said, there is still a JavaScript communication happening between your module and the client side in the browser. This means that handoff between the module and JavaScript can be hijacked the same way any other client-side code running in the browser can. These days most web applications are built defensively, but it can be easy to let our guard down and think that just because we're using a binary file instead of script that we're safe.

Any call that originates from inside your WebAssembly module can also originate from inside a debugger or from inside anything pretending to execute code on your behalf. For this reason, your back-end services supporting your WebAssembly module should be just as secure as they would be supporting regular Angular or React applications. One fairly easy to execute task is to download the WebAssembly module, disassemble it, alter the code, recompile it, and then re-inject it into the browser via proxy. If there's anything you wouldn't want executed in this scenario, you'll want to require credentials or some other form of checking for legitimate requests.

I am not a security expert, so I typically adopt a pattern I refer to as "Paranoia-Driven Development" (PDD). I make the assumption that every asset that can be downloaded from my site can be captured, altered, and used in a malicious or unexpected fashion. There are tools that can be used to ensure that scripts haven't been modified in transit, but even those can be defeated by people with enough determination and tools.

Signing and Encrypting WebAssembly Modules

In the previous section I talked about taking a paranoia approach to defense against external client tampering with WebAssembly modules. The consequences for module tampering can be far, far worse if you're distributing and using modules within your data center, cloud, or enterprise.

Let's say you've adopted WebAssembly and you're running some form of FaaS (Functions as a Service) infrastructure. Everything is great and you're loving the ease and portability you get, and you love the nearly crash-proof nature of running an interpreter on WebAssembly modules.

What if someone were to manage to slip a bad WebAssembly module into the environment. If your host protocol allows those modules to do things that could corrupt data, download data, or make outbound network calls, you could have all sorts of malicious actors controlling your system. What we need is some way to ensure the digital provenance of WebAssembly modules

—to ensure that they haven't been tampered with and that they were created by only authorized personnel or processes.

We can use *cryptographic signatures* to handle this problem. A simple hash of an array of bytes will allow us to tell if a file has been tampered with. We see this pattern used all the time on public downloads when the official sites also publish a checksum so you can verify that the file is legitimate.

A cryptographic signature takes that concept one step further. It produces a value that will not only change if the source file bytes change, but it is entirely dependent on some asymmetric, private key. In other words, you have to be in possession of a very carefully guarded secret in order to produce a valid signature.

Before your host code—whether it's a browser or a Rust console application or an OpenFaaS container—executes any code in a WebAssembly module, it should *verify* the signature that accompanies the file. If the verification fails, then the party who signed that file was not in posession of the right key and you should not only reject the file, but probably create some form of alert to trigger an investigation.

There are quite a few techniques to sign an array of bytes, but I am particularly partial to using Ed25519[2] keys. They're fast, simple, easy to use, and generally less vulnerable to certain types of attacks that have caused havoc in the past. There are more mathematical reasons to like this signature algorithm that I won't go into here because they make my head hurt.

With the *EdDSA* signature algorithm, you use a single private key called the *seed* key to sign an arbitrary binary payload. You can then use public keys generated from the *seed* to verify that signature. The availability of many public keys for a single binary key often creates some very powerful and elegant security solutions.

In this small Rust example (also included with the book code downloads), I illustrate using the signatory and signatory-dalek crates to sign and verify the contents of a WebAssembly file passed as the first argument on the command line:

signer/src/main.rs
```
use std::env;
use std::fs::File;
use std::io::prelude::*;

use signatory::{ed25519, Encode};
use signatory_dalek::{Ed25519Signer, Ed25519Verifier};
```

---

2. tools.ietf.org/html/rfc8032

```rust
fn main() -> Result<(), std::io::Error> {
    let args: Vec<String> = env::args().collect();
    let path = &args[1];

    let mut file = File::open(path)?;
    let mut wasm_buf = Vec::new();
    let _bytes_read = file.read_to_end(&mut wasm_buf)?;
    let buf: &[u8] = &wasm_buf;

    let seed = ed25519::Seed::generate();
    let base64 = signatory::encoding::Base64 {};
    println!(
        "Generated a seed/private key: {}",
        seed.encode_to_string(&base64).unwrap()
    );
    let signer = Ed25519Signer::from(&seed);

    let sig = ed25519::sign(&signer, buf).unwrap();
    println!(
        "Signature for {} created: {}",
        path,
        sig.encode_to_string(&base64).unwrap()
    );

    let pk = ed25519::public_key(&signer).unwrap();
    let verifier = Ed25519Verifier::from(&pk);

    let verified = ed25519::verify(&verifier, buf, &sig).is_ok();
    println!("Signature verified: {}", verified);

    Ok(())
}
```

Here's a sample run of the application:

```
$ target/debug/signer ../checkers/checkers.wasm
Generated a seed/private key: AOdRsk3TwSMO4chzRv4+EvXoGPuP25eMughoBRIGoKw=
Signature for ../checkers/checkers.wasm created:
wzphNwHoiPJvgooU8j36H0t8M4DjJ5Q0jyAbRPmIAmqZw+mBYG2dfCLgvCLd1b66
qGncRQkOUfhcAbaO7oqvBw==
Signature verified: true
```

The hard part with signing files isn't really the encryption code—others have already done the hard work for us by writing re-usable libraries. The difficulty with signatures is ensuring that the signature always accompany the file being signed.

There are a number of ways to do this. You could put the signature at the beginning of the binary file and then parse that out as you read it, treating the remainder of the binary file as the regular WebAssembly module. This has an added advantage of ensuring that the signature will never be apart from a file. This works because we know that ed25519 signatures are always 64 bytes, so we can simply read a fixed number of bytes from the beginning of the file.

I've coded up a sample (not refactored for cleanliness) that illustrates how to read a WebAssembly file, generate a signature from it, embed that signature in an output file, and then verify that the signature from a file matches the WebAssembly bytes—all of the tasks you would need to know how to do in order to secure the provenance of your modules. I'm only using base 64 encoding so I can print the signature out to the console:

```rust
signer2/src/main.rs
use std::env;
use std::fs::File;
use std::io::prelude::*;
use std::io::BufReader;

use signatory::{ed25519, Encode};
use signatory_dalek::{Ed25519Signer, Ed25519Verifier};

fn main() -> std::io::Result<()> {
    let args: Vec<String> = env::args().collect();

    let input = &args[1];
    let output = &args[2];

    let infile = load_file(input)?;
    let inbytes: &[u8] = &infile;
    let base64 = signatory::encoding::Base64 {};

    // This seed is a private key - store this in a safe place,
    // Obviously, you'll want to persist this somewhere instead of
    // just using it once in memory...
    let seed = ed25519::Seed::generate();
    let signer = Ed25519Signer::from(&seed);
    let sig = ed25519::sign(&signer, inbytes).unwrap();
    let sig_encoded = sig.encode_to_string(&base64).unwrap();

    let pk = ed25519::public_key(&signer).unwrap();
    let verifier = Ed25519Verifier::from(&pk);

    {
        let mut out_file = File::create(output)?;
        out_file.write(sig.as_bytes())?;
        out_file.write_all(inbytes)?;
    }

    println!(
        "Embedded signature into {} - output {}\n\t-->{}",
        input, output, sig_encoded
    );
```

```
    let mut sigbuf = [0; 64];
    let mut wasmbuf = vec![];
    {
        let in_file = File::open(output)?;
        let mut br = BufReader::new(in_file);
        br.read_exact(&mut sigbuf)?;
        br.read_to_end(&mut wasmbuf)?;
    }

    let wasmbytes: &[u8] = &wasmbuf;
    let insig = ed25519::Signature::new(sigbuf);

    let verify_res = ed25519::verify(&verifier, wasmbytes, &insig).is_ok();
    println!("Verification result on new bytes - {}", verify_res);

    Ok(())
}

fn load_file(path: &str) -> std::io::Result<Vec<u8>> {
    let mut file = File::open(path)?;
    let mut buf = Vec::new();
    let _bytes_read = file.read_to_end(&mut buf)?;

    Ok(buf)
}
```

You could also use this same embedding technique to add additional metadata to your WebAssembly file that might come from your build process or developers. Or, you could wrap the WebAssembly module bytes in a protocol buffer[3] binary file with fields for both raw bytes and a signature, which would save you the trouble of manually reading and writing custom binary file formats as you could just re-use the protocol buffer libraries available.

---

3. developers.google.com/protocol-buffers

Index

Thank you!

How did you enjoy this book? Please let us know. Take a moment and email us at support@pragprog.com with your feedback. Tell us your story and you could win free ebooks. Please use the subject line "Book Feedback."

Ready for your next great Pragmatic Bookshelf book? Come on over to https://pragprog.com and use the coupon code BUYANOTHER2019 to save 30% on your next ebook.

Void where prohibited, restricted, or otherwise unwelcome. Do not use ebooks near water. If rash persists, see a doctor. Doesn't apply to *The Pragmatic Programmer* ebook because it's older than the Pragmatic Bookshelf itself. Side effects may include increased knowledge and skill, increased marketability, and deep satisfaction. Increase dosage regularly.

And thank you for your continued support,

Andy Hunt, Publisher

SAVE 30%!
Use coupon code
BUYANOTHER2019

Practical Security

Most security professionals don't have the words "security" or "hacker" in their job title. Instead, as a developer or admin you often have to fit in security alongside your official responsibilities — building and maintaining computer systems. Implement the basics of good security now, and you'll have a solid foundation if you bring in a dedicated security staff later. Identify the weaknesses in your system, and defend against the attacks most likely to compromise your organization, without needing to become a trained security professional.

Roman Zabicki

(132 pages) ISBN: 9781680506341. $26.95

https://pragprog.com/book/rzsecur

Small, Sharp Software Tools

The command-line interface is making a comeback. That's because developers know that all the best features of your operating system are hidden behind a user interface designed to help average people use the computer. But you're not the average user, and the CLI is the most efficient way to get work done fast. Turn tedious chores into quick tasks: read and write files, manage complex directory hierarchies, perform network diagnostics, download files, work with APIs, and combine individual programs to create your own workflows. Put down that mouse, open the CLI, and take control of your software development environment.

Brian P. Hogan

(200 pages) ISBN: 9781680502961. $38.95

https://pragprog.com/book/bhcldev

Genetic Algorithms and Machine Learning for Programmers

Self-driving cars, natural language recognition, and online recommendation engines are all possible thanks to Machine Learning. Now you can create your own genetic algorithms, nature-inspired swarms, Monte Carlo simulations, cellular automata, and clusters. Learn how to test your ML code and dive into even more advanced topics. If you are a beginner-to-intermediate programmer keen to understand machine learning, this book is for you.

Frances Buontempo
(234 pages) ISBN: 9781680506204. $45.95
https://pragprog.com/book/fbmach

The Ray Tracer Challenge

Brace yourself for a fun challenge: build a photorealistic 3D renderer from scratch! It's easier than you think. In just a couple of weeks, build a ray tracer that renders beautiful scenes with shadows, reflections, brilliant refraction effects, and subjects composed of various graphics primitives: spheres, cubes, cylinders, triangles, and more. With each chapter, implement another piece of the puzzle and move the renderer that much further forward. Do all of this in whichever language and environment you prefer, and do it entirely test-first, so you know it's correct. Recharge yourself with this project's immense potential for personal exploration, experimentation, and discovery.

Jamis Buck
(290 pages) ISBN: 9781680502718. $45.95
https://pragprog.com/book/jbtracer

Programming Phoenix 1.4

Don't accept the compromise between fast and beautiful: you can have it all. Phoenix creator Chris McCord,
Elixir creator José Valim, and award-winning author
Bruce Tate walk you through building an application
that's fast and reliable. At every step, you'll learn from
the Phoenix creators not just what to do, but why.
Packed with insider insights and completely updated
for Phoenix 1.4, this definitive guide will be your constant companion in your journey from Phoenix novice
to expert, as you build the next generation of web applications.

Chris McCord, Bruce Tate and José Valim
(325 pages) ISBN: 9781680502268. $45.95
https://pragprog.com/book/phoenix14

Functional Web Development with Elixir, OTP, and Phoenix

Elixir and Phoenix are generating tremendous excite-
ment as an unbeatable platform for building modern
web applications. For decades OTP has helped developers create incredibly robust, scalable applications with
unparalleled uptime. Make the most of them as you
build a stateful web app with Elixir, OTP, and Phoenix.
Model domain entities without an ORM or a database.
Manage server state and keep your code clean with
OTP Behaviours. Layer on a Phoenix web interface
without coupling it to the business logic. Open doors
to powerful new techniques that will get you thinking
about web development in fundamentally new ways.

Lance Halvorsen
(218 pages) ISBN: 9781680502435. $45.95
https://pragprog.com/book/lhelph

Programming Elm

Elm brings the safety and stability of functional pro-
graming to front-end development, making it one of
the most popular new languages. Elm's functional nature and static typing means that run-time errors are
nearly impossible, and it compiles to JavaScript for
easy web deployment. This book helps you take advantage of this new language in your web site development.
Learn how the Elm Architecture will help you create
fast applications. Discover how to integrate Elm with
JavaScript so you can update legacy applications. See
how Elm tooling makes deployment quicker and easier.

Jeremy Fairbank
(250 pages) ISBN: 9781680502855. $40.95
https://pragprog.com/book/jfelm

React for Real

When traditional web development techniques don't
cut it, try React. Use React to create highly interactive
web pages faster and with fewer errors. With a little
JavaScript experience under your belt, you'll be up
and running in no time creating dynamic web applications. Craft isolated components that make your apps
easier to develop and maintain, with plenty of guidance
on best practices. Set up automated tests, and make
pages render fast for your users. See how to use your
React skills to integrate with other front-end technologies when needed.

Ludovico Fischer
(118 pages) ISBN: 9781680502633. $26.95
https://pragprog.com/book/lfreact

The Pragmatic Bookshelf

The Pragmatic Bookshelf features books written by developers for developers. The titles continue the well-known Pragmatic Programmer style and continue to garner awards and rave reviews. As development gets more and more difficult, the Pragmatic Programmers will be there with more titles and products to help you stay on top of your game.

Visit Us Online

This Book's Home Page
https://pragprog.com/book/khrust
Source code from this book, errata, and other resources. Come give us feedback, too!

Keep Up to Date
https://pragprog.com
Join our announcement mailing list (low volume) or follow us on twitter @pragprog for new titles, sales, coupons, hot tips, and more.

New and Noteworthy
https://pragprog.com/news
Check out the latest pragmatic developments, new titles and other offerings.

Save on the eBook

Save on the eBook versions of this title. Owning the paper version of this book entitles you to purchase the electronic versions at a terrific discount.

PDFs are great for carrying around on your laptop—they are hyperlinked, have color, and are fully searchable. Most titles are also available for the iPhone and iPod touch, Amazon Kindle, and other popular e-book readers.

Buy now at *https://pragprog.com/coupon*

Contact Us

Online Orders:	*https://pragprog.com/catalog*
Customer Service:	*support@pragprog.com*
International Rights:	*translations@pragprog.com*
Academic Use:	*academic@pragprog.com*
Write for Us:	*http://write-for-us.pragprog.com*
Or Call:	+1 800-699-7764

9 781680 506365